AN AMERICA THAT WAS

An America That Was

WHAT LIFE WAS LIKE ON AN ILLINOIS FARM SEVENTY YEARS AGO

by Albert Britt

BARRE PUBLISHERS

BARRE, MASSACHUSETTS

1964

THANKS ARE TENDERED
TO THE MEMBERS OF MR.
McCutcheon's family,
THE CHICAGO TRIBUNE,
THE CHICAGO HISTORICAL
SOCIETY AND THE NEW-
BERRY LIBRARY FOR USE
OF THE JOHN T. McCut-
CHEON DRAWINGS USED
IN THIS BOOK.

I would be remiss if I did not acknowl-
edge the form and focus given to this
book by Thea Wheelwright who superbly
edited my manuscript.

Albert Britt
Wellington Farm
Nonquit, Mass.

Copyright © by Albert Britt
All Rights Reserved
Composed and Printed in the United States of America
Library of Congress Catalog Number: 64-14906

To the grandchildren

Molly, Elizabeth, Peter and Joy

That they, too, may know
The way by which we came

C 1   MAR 1 2 1965

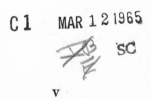 SC

v

CONTENTS

FOREWORD

I HAVE long had a dream about a lovely land. There are neither television sets nor aeroplanes there, and no one fears fall-out or the supersonic missile with atomic warhead, because neither has been created yet and, if all goes well, never will be. Nor is anyone making arrangements to blast off for the moon, trying to bounce a radio signal off some inoffensive star, or telephoning the police to report the theft of 17 credit cards from the glove compartment of his unpaid-for auto.

People do not hurry in my country. They stop to chat when they meet someone they know, instead of muttering a mechanical "Hi!" as they scurry past, intent on some useless electronic-age errand. (Such meetings always happen on a tree-shaded street with a small child nearby doing a brisk business in lemonade.) There are no paved highways, either; no billboards, no disc jockeys. If wonder drugs and electric refrigerators are unknown, so too are the memory of storm troopers and Little Rock and several world wars.

In fact my dreamland is a sort of demi-Paradise, basking in fresh air and sunshine, instead of smothered with smoke, exhaust fumes and industrial waste; echoing to the singing of birds and the clop-clop of horses' hooves, rather than to the roar of traffic and the sound of a jukebox playing the same tune over and over and over . . .

Now comes *An America That Was*, and to my delight that shimmering land turns out not to have been imaginary after all. I was thinking, it seems, of rural Illinois as it was some three-quarters of a century ago, although even my most convincing dreams lack the clarity and dimension of the record set down by Albert Britt of how it was in those less-encumbered days.

Like a traveler returning from some inaccesible area which only he, among all outlanders, has been able to reach, Britt recalls its geography and its people. Through his eyes you see the winding roads, the waving grass, the barren towpaths and the little schoolhouses. You become familiar with McGuffey's Readers and the need to break the ice in the pitcher before washing yourself on winter mornings. You share the universal fear of night air breathed as you sleep. You discover such outmoded virtues as make-do, think-for-yourself, and help-thy-neighbor. Doctors come when summoned, at any hour and in any weather; the bread is home-baked and crusty, wild berries are sweet, and the world—your world at least—is all in order, instead of being a jigsaw puzzle which has as many players taking it to pieces as it has trying to put it together.

An America That Was is an incredibly skillful job of re-creating a period of our nation's history which long ago slid into the mist, and of peopling it with the proper characters. Britt is a secret agent who makes his way from behind the curtain of time with a report accurate to the most unimportant crossroad, the manner of speech, even the names the women gave to their patchwork patterns. He is a magician who waves his hand, mutters an incantation, and the landscape changes: animals, trees, buildings, high-roads, scents and sounds appear as they haven't been since Huck Finn's day.

As you read it, his countryside becomes one you learn well enough to pass as a native in, if such a chance were offered, and you may develop that I've-been-here-before feeling, so perfectly does Britt weave into a comprehensive whole all the isolated details you may have remembered regularly.

Even for those too young to share his memories, *An America That Was* is an absorbing story of life in rustic and smalltown Illinois only 20 years or so after the Civil War. It is prefaced by a convincing picture of who settled the region and why they came there to satisfy their hunger for land.

The book is filled with revealing glimpses: the winning word in a spelling bee, the sputtering surprise of a small boy who discovers that cistern water can be icy even on a summer's night, the wedding celebration known as a "shivaree". There is the dusty drudgery of harvest time, the communal excitement of raising a barn, the fun of an overnight visit from your best friends, the fascination of the general store. There are the forgotten dangers of diphtheria (we've substituted the high-speed crash), and the feeling of a scene unrolling slowly, with plenty of time to watch the parade, rather than flashing by like something glimpsed from a rocketing express train.

It gave me great pleasure to read *An America That Was*. I am indebted for this proof that my dreamland once existed and that it was, apparently, as much sport to live there as I always suspected it would be.

May I welcome you to an enchanting place—the boyhood of Albert Britt.

Robert Cromie

INTRODUCTION

THE PERIOD from 1875 to 1900 lies in a twilight zone of history to the Americans of today. Old ways were changing then, but men still thought as their fathers had, and no one could guess the depth of the revolution that was upon us. The Civil War was behind us, but men still in their middle years could tell first hand stories of the third day at Gettysburg or the trenches around Petersburg. There were seven presidential campaigns in that quarter of a century, and in all but two the successful candidate had been an officer in the Union Army. Grover Cleveland was the exception, and a favorite argument against him had been that he sent a substitute. A proposal to return the captured Confederate battle flags had provoked a storm of opposition in Congress. New issues were appearing, but they were easily avoided until the closing years of the century.

Industrial wealth was growing, but west of the Alleghenies we still thought of ourselves as an agrarian people, which we were. The West was filling up, but homesteaders could still find virgin land in eastern Kansas and Nebraska, and the Dakotas did not become states until 1889. Sitting Bull wiped out Custer's command on the Little Big Horn in 1876, and even fourteen years after that, at Wounded Knee, the irreconcilable old savage staked his life on the power of his Ghost Dancers to bring back the dead warriors and the vanished buffalo. The menace of the Apaches in the Southwest was not ended until 1886 when Geronimo surrendered.

The old frontier had frayed out in the wide spaces of the High Plains, but the log cabin still had its usefulness as the birthplace of candidates, and pioneering times were active memories in the minds of living men. An argument for Garfield in the campaign of 1880 was that he had driven mules on the towpath of an Ohio canal to earn the money to take him to college. Farmers were proud of their new and improved machinery then as they are now, but the horse set the pace and fixed the dimensions within which the farmers lived. Five or six miles from home found them among strangers. There were railroads and telegraph lines, but men and news traveled slowly. The election of a sheriff was often more important than the choice of a President. The American home was closer in form and feeling to the past than to the incredible future that was in the making.

Remote as those days seem now, they were the living reality to men and women who are still alive. Historians are traversing that time and embalming it in pages of analysis and interpretation in which ordinary people tend to disappear. What was it like to live then? Statisticians can construct tables and graphs of change, but tables and graphs are lifeless things. How did the times appear to people living in the midst of them? What did those people do to live, and how? What did they read? How did they talk, and about what? What was the country school to the youngsters who sat on the hard benches? McGuffey's Readers and Webster's blue-backed spelling book were fading but not yet gone. What was the country church before it became a curiosity? How did people amuse themselves with no radios to turn on or moving pictures to look at in a nearby town? How could one live without telephones, electric lights, automobiles, or even typewriters?

In any attempt to recreate that America, so remote and still so near, it is inevitable that personal pronouns should creep in. What follows is an attempt to give form and life to ways and people that are fast fading out of the memories of living men. What may seem like an autobiography is really nothing of the sort. People lived then and worked and played and dreamed as other people do now. This is an account of life in An America That Was by a participant in that life. I was young then and this was the way it seemed to me. ALBERT BRITT

CHAPTER I

The Town That Wasn't There

I WAS BORN in a town that didn't exist, although it had a
name; it was called Utah, Illinois, but it will not be found on
highway maps. Nevertheless I was born there, a place that wasn't
there. The explanation lies in an almost forgotten bit of American
history. When railroads began to take the place of stagecoaches
as regular carriers of the mail, there were many large areas remote
from railroad points that could be reached only by country carriers, and the postal authorities were forced to make provisions
for them. The routes traveled by carriers on horseback or in
old-fashioned buggies were marked on postal maps with stars and
known as Star Routes. Utah was on one of those country routes.
To me it was a farmhouse owned by John Landon, a local Republican stalwart, Civil War veteran, perennial town clerk, casual
farmer, and postmaster, but to the postal authorities in Washington he was Utah.

With the beginning of rural free delivery in 1896, the stars
began to fade and now they are forgotten, but while they shone,
however uncertainly in times when our roads were even worse
than usual, they were our sole link with the outside world, weekly
proof that there was a federal government.

The Star Routes had some unpleasant publicity in the early
eighties. The government dealt through contractors who were
supposed to bid for the contract to carry the mail on several routes
and to take the responsibility for hiring and firing carriers. Investigation revealed the embarrassing fact that sometimes the competi-

1

tion of bidders was pure illusion and that some contractors were charging for carrying the mail over routes that didn't exist. Circumstances pointed to collusion in Washington and a few minor rascals went to jail. Technicalities of jurisdiction and procedure saved the big boys.

Geographically the farm where I was born was in Kelly Township, Warren County, Illinois. The minute rectangle that represents our first eighty acres was described in the deed as the "East half of the Northeast quarter of section Twenty-nine in Township Twelve North, Range One, West of the Fourth Principal Meridian in the tract appropriated for Military Bounties in the Territory of Illinois."[1] There's an important paragraph of our national history wrapped up in that surveyor's riddle. The solution is to be found in "An Ordinance for ascertaining the mode of disposing of Lands in the Western Territory." This law, passed by the Continental Congress, May 20, 1785, was one of the wisest bits of legislation in our long list of statutory experiments. The survey system it lays down makes possible the easy location of a piece of land and simplifies the process of purchase and transfer. The method in use in the old colonies was a combination of counting one's steps along a boundary suited to the contour of the land, with considerable reliance on hearsay and guesswork.

The old law of 1785 marked the appearance of our Uncle Sam as a real-estate operator on a large scale. The colonies claiming charter grants of western land had ceded their claims to the Congress during the Revolution, and now that body was taking

[1]Probably the reference to Military Bounties needs translation. When the Revolution ended, the treasury of the new government was empty and the continental currency was virtually worthless. The soldiers gave the ragged paper away, a month's pay for a pair of boots, a night's lodging, a dram of rum, anything that they could get. Many of them realized nothing. After the War of 1812, the government took steps to pay the debt to the soldiers and sailors. There was plenty of raw land in the new west, and Congress voted to set aside the large triangle between the Illinois and Mississippi rivers to be deeded to the veterans or their heirs or assigns. This was long known as the Military Tract, and the counties formed therein were named for officers of the Revolution, and the War of 1812: Knox, Warren, Henderson, McDonough, Stark and the like.

the first step in providing for the sale of the land to prospective settlers—and speculators too, as the near future was to prove. Whoever wrote that ordinance—Jefferson must have had a hand in it—was concerned with an inventory of natural resources as well as with survey systems and maps. The surveyor was instructed to note on his plat, "at their proper distances, all mines, salt-springs, saltlicks, and millseats that shall come to his knowledge, and all watercourses, mountains, and other remarkable things, over and near which such lines shall pass, and also the quality of the lands."[2]

Our own farm was old for Illinois. The original eighty was the east half of a quarter section that was deeded to "Israel T. Houghton, father and heir-at-law of Washington Houghton deceased, late a corporal in Lytle's Company, Fourth Rifle Company," evidently one of the sharpshooters and a casualty of the War of 1812. The date of the instrument was 1817, the year before Illinois became a state. That deed bears the signature of James Monroe, then President. The prudent Israel, a resident in Woodstock, Vermont, seems to have had no appetite for western adventure, for on the back of the document can still be deciphered a bill of sale to Charles Dana, also of Woodstock, for the sum of one hundred dollars, two months after the issuance of deed number one. How many times the land was sold before the first settler appeared on it I do not know, but it is of record that the first settler came into the county in 1827. In the years between 1815 and 1830 there was brisk speculation in deeds and bounty certificates for Western land that none of the parties to the trading ever saw.

The year of my birth was properly inscribed in the family Bible as 1874, but family talk was likely to identify it as "the year before the cyclone." That was an event for which our family, eight in number, had front seats. Clum Robison's forty acres of timber was only a quarter of a mile from our house. In a few seconds what

[2]The Land Ordinance of 1785 applied chiefly to Virginia, Connecticut, Massachusetts, and the Carolinas. The new feature of the ordinance was the provision for a survey system with a "section" of 640 acres as the basic unit; townships to be of equal size, six miles square, "as near as may be"; Section Number 16 in each township to be set aside for the support of public schools.

had been a fine stand of growing trees was a tangled swath of down timber two hundred yards wide. Trees two or three feet in diameter were twisted by the incredible wind or uprooted and thrown down in hopeless confusion. What had been green life was changed in a fraction of a minute to desolation and death, much of it to remain for years as a reminder of a second or two of whirling chaos. Only a Lafcadio Hearn could describe the work of a cyclone.

After the eccentric manner of its kind our violent visitor took off at that point in a long leap, touching the earth again seven or eight miles to the eastward, where it tossed the tiny village of Soperville about like a child's building blocks. I might claim to have seen the cyclone, since family tradition assures me that Father held me in an anxious grasp, ready to run in any direction that promised a chance of safety. There was then no cellar under our small house. We came through, but a margin of four hundred yards is slender insurance.

The choosing of the cyclone as a dating point in our chronology was characteristic of the way of simple people living isolated lives. Years and seasons came and blended into a stream of other months and years, but cyclones and births and marriages and deaths and other forms of calamity were not to be forgotten. We had almanacs, of course, important items in a meager family library, supplementing the Bible and a Webster, considerably abridged. We needed few words for our daily communications. The almanac I remember best was Ayer's. In addition to containing the usual monthly tables, with Sundays and holidays printed in red, it gave us exciting facts such as the signs of the Zodiac, with the conventional symbols for Taurus, Gemini, Pisces, and the rest; standard treatment for distemper and nosebleed; the right way to deal with boils; small anecdotes wih highly moral implications; bits of verse, and of course weather forecasts for a year ahead. Some of these were almost right, thanks to a calculated vagueness in the prophecy and a charitable willingness to believe on the part of the reader.

This was the America of the frying pan and the deep fear of

night air, hence our almanac made frequent reference to sarsaparilla, an all-purpose tonic warranted to cure all ills, present or future, that was Mr. Ayer's chief reason for existing. If we doubted we had only to read the testimonials that he offered, an impressive number of them signed by clergymen. The rule of these medicine men was to claim everything in the confident expectation that some of it would stick; and it worked for a long time.

Our neighbors were typical of early Illinois farm communities, predominantly of New York, New England, and Virginia origin, with later additions from English, Irish, and Swedish sources. Family records and old deeds show that the name of Adcock was one of the early ones written on the farms around us. Virginia was the starting point for the Adcocks' westward thrust, following the route taken by the Lincolns, probably through Cumberland Gap, pausing briefly in Kentucky, then across the Ohio into Indiana and so to Illinois, always looking for more and better land and a place where there were fewer neighbors.

Southern Illinois is still a region of southern speech, southern ways, and southern sympathies. At the time of the Civil War these counties inclined strongly toward secession and sent many men into Confederate armies. In later years I was to hear men in coal towns there speak of sheriffs, county prosecutors and chiefs of police as "the Law." "Then the Law came in." It was thus that moonshiners in southern mountains spoke of "revenuers." When the motorist driving south through Illinois reaches a point where townships no longer exist as political or administrative units, he may know that there the South begins. After the War of 1812 migrants from New England and eastern New York moved as near due west as primitive roads and waterways would permit, and the township, born in New England, traveled with them.

Jacksonville, Illinois, near Springfield, was near the southern boundary of this belt, and its early population was a blending of New England and the South. Adcocks came there soon and in the early thirties three Adcock brothers, Henry, Edmund, and Case, set out from the infant settlement of Jacksonville, following up the Illinois and its tributaries, looking for wild honey and land where there was elbow room. In due course their wanderings brought them to Kelly Township, then only Township Twelve on a surveyor's map, and there they stayed, taking up land on the edge of a broad belt of wooded, broken country. This was an ideal location in the eyes of the early comers, with in one direction the beginning of the prairie, with few trees to interfere with the plow, and in the other, dense woods to provide fuel, material for fences and buildings, and shelter from winter storms, the familiar environment of the older states. Open prairie was a new landscape to men born among the trees, rocks and rivers of the East, and one to be approached with caution, for how could man live without trees and running water?

One of the old Adcock homes is remembered by me with special pleasure. I knew it first as the home of Robert, son of Henry of the bee hunting trio. It was old, the original part of it built by one Atwood in 1828, probably the oldest house in the county. Atwood had moved on in 1833, five years after his arrival, because with other houses appearing around Cameron ten miles away the country was becoming too crowded. The living room with its low ceiling, wide fireplace, and a "nightcap cupboard" over the mantelpiece hinted at the secure and leisurely life of an older settlement somewhere east or south. A hundred yards away was the family burying ground, a small square cleared of trees and fenced in to keep livestock away, a reminder of colonial Virginia practice that was repeated on each of the original Adcock home farms. House and farm are still owned by a member of the family, a great grandson of Henry. Five generations in the line of ownership is not a bad record. Not all Americans spend their lives on the road.

It should be added that the claustrophobic Atwood had enclosed his house in a stockade containing a spring of cold clear water in case of Indian attack. There is no trace of spring or stockade, but the old house stands. The village that Black Hawk fought to keep was only fifty miles away, and the winding road that passed the house, once called the Military Road, was one of the trails over which militia marched to the hunting of Black Hawk and his warriors. It is not impossible that young Abraham Lincoln, newly elected captain of militia, traveled that road on his way to the war that he never quite caught up with.

The early settlers were of the older breeds that had taken and held the early states. Not far away, clustered around the sleepy village of Henderson, were families with such names as Robertson, Henderson, McMurtree, reminiscent of the Scotch Highlanders in the mountains of North Carolina and Tennessee. They were a lively, hospitable people, good shots, lovers of horses and dogs, not averse to a small bet on a cockfight or an impromptu horse race or wrestling match, scandalizing some of the more straitlaced citizens. But they were good farmers, friendly neighbors, and Democrats to a man. Beneath their surface of lively gaiety were integrity, courage and purpose.

There is a characteristic footnote to the chronicles of that day. Soon there appeared, a few miles south of Henderson, a group of serious, determined, pious people bent on the founding of a college, a church, and a community. In their plan there was no place for the sort of gaiety that Henderson found agreeable and harmless. Hard on their heels came a Yankee merchant looking for a place to open a general store. He cast a critical and discerning eye over both hamlets, now emerging from the log cabin stage, and reached a swift conclusion. Serious people who stay home nights and go to church on Sundays save their money and pay their bills, said he to himself. Henderson may have more fun, but the other crowd will have more cash customers. At least so he made his choice, with little subsequent occasion for regret. Was it Parkman who made caustic comment on the ability of the Puritans to combine piety and profit?

The westward tide was running fast in the thirties of that century, and other families came close behind the Adcocks from other parts of the older America, drawn by the same lure of free land.

Mingled with Adcocks were Terpenings, Townsends, Wallaces, and Sallees, all English by way of the older colonies. Armstrongs came from the north of Ireland, sturdy, God-fearing Protestants, to intermarry with older Americans, clear land, and build houses that grew with the growth of the family.

Much of the Middle West was settled in this random fashion. Families of diverse backgrounds came from widely separated points in the more crowded East, without plan or previous agreement. They were mostly young, few had capital, and none had bank accounts or credit except as the land they sought gave it to them. The decade of the thirties was one of the big ones in the records of our westward wandering. Public land office records show that in the good years before the speculative bubble burst in 1837, new farms were appearing north of the Ohio at the rate of twenty thousand a year. Farms, mind you, not towns or villages. These people were looking for land that would soon earn the dollar and a quarter an acre that it cost them. The growing mill towns of the North Atlantic States were clamoring for laborers and paying good wages by Old World standards, but these people proposed to work for themselves. The midwest democracy, owning itself and its land, was taking shape.

My own family was English, straight from Sussex, back of Hastings. Father had first tried his lot in "York State," landing in New York out of the steerage of a sailing ship in 1853, twenty-three years old, with less than a hundred dollars in his pocket and none at all anywhere else. One of the few heirlooms that I possess of that stage in our family Odyssey is the two-tined bone-handled fork that with a pocket knife, a tin plate, and a cup constituted his cutlery in the crowded, badly ventilated quarters that he shared with other hopeful immigrants in the five weeks of westward sailing. Edward Brett was one of the large number of landless Englishmen of that day, without trade of status. Barring a few months in a dame school, he was self-educated. The school was taught by an old woman in her own small cottage and offered only the simplest rudiments of reading, writing and arithmetic. As education it was scanty enough, but it was the best that thousands of children from English lower class families could have, and better than that which many others received.

Did the Iron Duke really say that Waterloo was won on the playing fields of Eton and Harrow? If he did it was with his tongue in his cheek—or else he was a fool, and he was never that. Napoleon was beaten by soldiers many of whom could neither read nor write, and the old duke knew it. Privately he damned his soldiers as the sweepings of the London streets and described the battle as a near thing. Sweepings or not, they held the British squares against what was still the best army in Europe, and that was good enough.

My feeling about England is darkened by my knowledge of her long and shameful neglect of English men and women. It should be said for Edward Brett that on the slender foundation the Old Country gave him he built a good life, as a landholder and a respected citizen in a new world who gave each of his six children a better start than could have been dreamed of in the England of his day.

Why did he come to America, a far land and a strange one? For the same reason that most of the other immigrants came, for land. There was none to be had for purchase or for rent in England. There was land for wide estates, beautiful parks with noble oak trees and deer grazing in the shade, all very picturesque, but none for land-hungry Englishmen, the little fellows born on the wrong side of the neat hedges. The choice was between a bare living wage in Merrie England and land of his own in raw America. He chose America.

His first job was as a hired hand on a farm near a small town in New York State known to me only as Head of the River. It was somewhere beyond the Catskills back of Kingston on the Hudson. Among his memories of that time was a trip by stagecoach from the river to his destination. The driver was apparently a specimen of a *genus Americana* that has been widely prevalent in our history, the harmless liar. Among the playful prevarications with which he entertained his outside passengers was the recitation of some impressive lines of verse, "Breathes there a man with soul so dead/Who never to himself hath said/This is my own, my native land," which he modestly admitted having written. The young Englishman's knowledge of English literature was too scanty then for him to know that Walter Scott had written it first.

Father's only reason for choosing Head of the River as the place to stop was the fact that his brother Jim, who had come over a year earlier, was somewhere thereabouts. After some difficulty the brother was located by his colloquial name of English Jimmy. It was here that the spelling of the family name was changed from Brett to Britt. In England the vowel had been *E*, but the English being English, it was pronounced as though it were *I*. The result was confusion and annoyance to American ears. Why not pronounce it the way it was spelled? But the Bretts being English too, it was the spelling that was changed. It was as simple as that, a gentlemen's agreement between the brothers without benefit of court or law. Hardheaded old Grandfather Foster never recognized the alteration, and his letters to my mother were always addressed to Mrs. Edward Brett. No New World nonsense for him.

At Head of the River the new arrival soon found a job on a nearby farm. All that a hired man needed then was a strong back, the will to work, and the ability to acquire at least a speaking acquaintance with horses. Father had the back and the will, but he was always a trifle detached and casual in his dealings with horses, feeling much more at home on his own feet with axe or hoe in his hands. The saying that a westerner would walk half a mile to catch a horse to ride a quarter of a mile in the opposite direction never applied to him. Another American practice that he discovered along with the importance of the horse was that a hired man was regarded as a human being and a member of the family, at least at meal time.

Some time in the year before Father returned to England to be married, he and Jim decided to have a look farther west, as the land around Head of the River was well settled and high in price.

One of the regions where the brothers looked about was in western Illinois, south of Rock Island. That was and is a pleasant country of wooded land along the small rivers that feed the Mississippi, with belts of level prairie land between. Why they chose to try their fortunes in the little town of Oquawka on the Illinois side of the Mississippi, north of the larger town of Burlington in Iowa, I do not know, except that they found jobs there. Probably that was reason enough.

At that time the great river was still the main north and south highway and the towns along it were busy places. Great rafts of white pine logs floated downriver from the logging camps in Wisconsin to find the saws and planes to turn them into lumber for houses and towns. Dubuque, Galena, Clinton, Rock Island, Muscatine, New Boston, Oquawka, were working and growing and talking loudly of their imposing futures.

Oquawka was especially voluble on this point. When railroads began to creep across the state from and to Chicago in the early fifties, there was talk of a steel artery across Iowa to Omaha and beyond. Oquawka regarded this prospect with pleased complacency. There could be but one point where the line would cross the river, and that of course was Oquawka. Clearly the town was destined for greatness. It couldn't miss. The publisher of the local weekly set about planning a national magazine which would make his town a literary as well as a lumber center, another Athens of America. It is of record that an offer was made to Edgar Allan Poe to come out and be the editor. Poe's reply, if he made one, is unknown, but he did not come and there was no magazine.

The mortal blow was the decision by the builders of what is now the main line of the Chicago, Burlington and Quincy Railroad to cross at Burlington twenty miles to the south, leaving the budding metropolis to her dreams beside the great river.

Whatever the future of the river towns, this one met the first need of the new Americans, jobs and a chance to save enough money to justify marriage and a serious beginning as citizens and landholders.

CHAPTER II

First Steps in a New World

FOUR or five years of exploration and experiment in America had provided the immigrant with some understanding of the new land and a meager reserve of American gold, enough at least to encourage the next step, matrimony. There had been no talk of an engagement between himself and Sarah Foster. Working-class economy and codes of conduct had little room or money for anything so formal and expensive as betrothal. An understanding that Edward should go and Sarah should wait was the best they could contrive, but it endured the almost five years of separation. While he worked and saved and looked for land in the New World she worked and saved and waited in the Old, waitress, nurse, lady's maid. So the years passed.

There were gradations of status even at the working-class level and Sarah was perhaps a cut above her prospective husband in spite of going "out to service." Grandfather Foster was steward, estate manager, if one wants to make it sound better, for a Colonel Nicholls, a well-to-do Englishman who was something in the India service. The East India Company still had considerable remnants of its old power in that land and was to hold it until the Sepoy Rebellion in 1857 broke it for good. Part of a steward's emolument was the use of a house and walled garden, a solid square stone structure that still stands, unless a Nazi bomb erased it when the Luftwaffe paid their respects to the countryside back of Hastings. He was also clerk of the parish church at Mountfield, with the duty of saying Amen at appropriate points in the service.

Quite a fellow, my Grandfather Foster, with a stubborn will and a hard hand for the erring. As he grew older he was known as "Old Tom," but his broad shoulders and strong arms did not encourage undue familiarity. A village wag met him in the middle of a muddy crossing and eyed the old man's shaggy hair. Holding out sixpence, the joker advised Grandfather, "Go get your hair cut." The joke didn't quite come off. The huge right hand swung once and the rash young man was flat in the mud. Old Tom went his unruffled way unbarbered.

I grew up under the grim stare of his uncompromising eyes viewing me disapprovingly from a colored "crayon" enlargement of a tintype on our living-room wall, the work of one of the itinerant artists who used to travel country roads in the Middle West. In spite of the atrocious coloring and the ornate frame, he was an impressive figure, a piece of old Sussex, dressed in the country fashion of the day, with smock and gaiters, holding a gnarled stick cut from one of the Colonel's hedgerows.

He died when I was five or six years old, and of course I never saw him, but I have read some of his letters in his precise, angular hand, the lines carefully "crossed" on thin paper to save postage. He was appalled by the waste and slaughter of the Civil War and could see no future for America but poverty and struggle for years to come. "Come home," he urged repeatedly, offering to send the money to pay the passage for our growing family. I doubt if such an ignominious retreat was ever discussed as even a remote possibility. Wages were good and the land beckoned. The Britts were here to stay.

An English cousin once took me to see the old man's grave in the little churchyard at Mountfield and as I read the inscription ordered by his employer, "Well done, good and faithful servant," I felt my freeborn American soul writhe in quite unreasonable resentment. Service is an honorable estate, but why rub it in? The same cousin showed me another monument to Old Tom, a double row of great chestnut trees he had planted along the drive leading up from the highroad to the manor house, the latter a Georgian affair with wide grounds and gardens. That was a memorial to be prized.

As befitted a new American, a citizen in the making, and a bridegroom with a little money in his pocket, Father scorned the steerage on this his third crossing. In ocean travel in the year 1858, third class was better than steerage, but not by much. Mother never spoke of this voyage, her first glimpse of the world outside her narrow English orbit. Perhaps her impressions of her wedding trip were the kind that are gladly forgotten: rough seas, poor food, crowded quarters, slow travel, although the boat combined sail and steam. And there was a third member of the party, Martha Mepham, on her way out to marry Uncle Jim. Such a triangle holds large possibilities of discord. Whatever happened of pleasant companionship or otherwise, Mother's relations with her sister-in-law seemed always a trifle strained.

Once past the immigration officers in New York, the question of where to go was easily answered. Oquawka was the place. There jobs could be had for the asking and land not far away could be found when the time came. The heyday of the little river towns was soon to pass, but the mills were busy and another job was waiting. Of this period I know little. Hard-working people seldom dwell on past hardships. Life was expected to be hard, so why dramatize it in retrospect? Mother would sometimes refer feelingly to the hot nights and the swarming mosquitoes of a river town in midsummer, but even that was infrequent.

Another English family, the Forwards, had settled there and a close friendship grew up with them. The big event of what must have been my fourth year was a trip by train to visit the Forwards, but it was the train and not the Forwards that made it memorable. To country people in that day, railroad travel was a romantic adventure and telegrams, if any ever reached us, were heralds of tragedy. On my first trip the news butcher selling magazines, books, candy, apples, oranges, was my chief object of envy. To spend one's life on a train would be unalloyed bliss. Apples were commonplace to a farm child, and books and magazines were without meaning to me, but oranges were a luxury. More than once a

large orange was the sole tenant of my Christmas stocking. Our
family income provided plenty of good food and clothes enough,
always a "best" suit for Sundays, but there was scanty margin for
presents.

Jobs were still plentiful along the Mississippi when the Britts
landed in Oquawka in 1858, and the pay was good by English
standards, but it was land they wanted and soon, land and a home.
Where was it to be? By a combination of some searching, local
information, and plain luck, spurred on by their own desire, they
chose a spot in Warren County, some thiry miles east of Oquawka.
Thither they moved in March, 1859. The period of guessing
was ended.

The first farm home was a rented one, owned by a Captain
Kelly, late a captain in Her British Majesty's merchant marine.

My older sister Fanny was born on the Kelly farm, and in a
year or two the family moved to another rented farm whose better
soil gave promise of faster saving against the purchase of the
coveted place of our own. There four more children were born.
Children were assets then, not long-term liabilities. This second
home was near a crossroads with a name and a sense of particular
identity. This was Tylerville, according to local legend named
for President Tyler.

Tylerville deserves a small place in this chronicle of life in
an earlier America. It was a little more than a star on a postal
map and something less than a village. Partly by chance and partly
for the sake of neighbors, there was a house on or near each of the
four corners where two roads crossed. One of these was known to
me later as the Old Terpening house, one as the Bunker house. The
third was unnamed and the fourth housed the Britt family until
1869 when the long dream that had brought two immigrants across
the Atlantic came true and the Britts became landowners, eighty
acres at twenty-five dollars an acre.

The name of Terpening was repeated rather frequently
around Tylerville. The manner of their coming was typical of the
westward wandering of the time. The first of the name, John Peter,
came from Saratoga County, New York, drawn by reports of fer-

tile virgin soil to be had for little more than the asking. On his initial trip in 1835 to look the country over, he had traveled on foot from somewhere in Ohio. A year later he came again to stay, bringing with him not only a new wife but also his father and mother and, according to family records, nine brothers and sisters. This second trip was really devious, illustrating the travel difficulties of that day: the new Erie Canal to Buffalo, steamboat to Cleveland, canal again to Portsmouth on the Ohio, another steamboat down the Ohio and up the Mississippi to St. Louis, where ice delayed them for a month. New Years Day of 1837 saw them arriving at Quincy in Illinois after three months on the way, and still nearly two hundred long miles short of their destination. Quincy held them until spring when they rounded out their family Odyssey in a covered wagon. And what a family it was, Father Ezekiel and his wife, John P. and his bride Mindwell, five brothers and four sisters. The wagons of families, clans, and colonies were marking the land with wheelmarks where solitary frontiersmen had blazed trails.

The first Terpening farm had "improvements," in the language of the day, a house and stable, both of logs, and four acres of plowed land. The house was a single room, eighteen by twenty feet. Unless there had been unreported strays somewhere on the way, the Terpenings numbered thirteen at that time, all adults. To complete the congestion, the former owner, one Billup, was still there with a wife and ten children, and there they all stayed for three bleak March weeks while Billup's new house was having a roof put on. As an old man, John P. recalled those weeks: "We were thicker than three in a bed, as the floor, our only bed, was covered." Incredible? Of course, but it was so the old man remembered it in his eighties. Large families in small houses was the rule of the day.

All this was ancient history when the Britts arrived more than twenty years later, and Tylerville had acquired a name and something of an identity, but no exact boundaries or political form. It was, and still is, only a neighborhood. That its development was random and accidental is written in the record of what passed for community institutions. The first school had been opened in a log building nearly a mile away from the crossroads that was the tacit center of Tylerville, with the determined John P. as the teacher. Thence it had drifted to a frame structure, built for school purposes, only a quarter of a mile from the four corners, where it stood until 1880. Its final migration was to a point nearly three-quarters of a mile distant from the crossroads, and there it ended its days. Its fate is emblematic of the passing of the country school of sacred tradition. Building and school yard became the property of the owner of the farm land surrounding it, who by a species of obscure historic irony was my brother Charlie, once a teacher in the school.

The Tylerville Church (Methodist) has been more stable as a community center. The first religious services in the neighborhood were held in the log schoolhouse and started with the school on its wanderings, but in 1871 the church acquired a home of its own on the corner next to the old house that had housed us for a time. That was the church where I was early enrolled in Sunday School and where I dozed and fidgeted through sermons that I found both long and dull. It was well built in the manner of the time, with sills and frame cut from nearby timber and hewn by farmers skilled in the use of the adz and the broadaxe. Good trees went to the building. They had to be good to provide sills forty feet long and nine inches square. Such trees are things of the past, white oak fifty to a hundred years in the growing.

Around the grave of a Terpening daughter the Terpening burying ground developed, the final resting place of the forefathers of the community. It is still there, not far from the spot where the first Terpening settled. If there can be such a thing as an attractive cemetery this is it. The only attempts to beautify it are the flowers planted by sorrowing women. Now and again neighbors cut the grass and mend the fence and straighten the stones that mark the graves. Forest trees lean over it and wild flowers in the spring testify to the continuity of life and beauty.

Much later, in my own youth in fact, a crossroads store appeared in Tylerville, this time snug against the wagon tracks along which the customers came. That was also a Terpening enterprise, run by Harry, a part of that complicated web of sons, grandsons, nieces, nephews, cousins, aunts, and uncles of the clan that had multiplied since John P.'s considerable arrival in 1837.

Harry sold obvious groceries, tobacco, chewing gum, and cheap candy, a small stock of work clothes, and a limited amount of necessary implements and tools, axes, rakes, spades, hammers, wrenches, screwdrivers, and the like. Mostly he dealt in leisure and local gossip. Summer afternoons horseshoe pitching was likely to break out on a level spot behind the store when farm work was not too pressing, but Saturday evenings in the winter were the occasions. Unless a blizzard blocked the roads the regulars were always there, a game of checkers going not far from the hot stove, dominoes perhaps, but mostly talk, idle, inconsequential references to people and things known to the talkers.

Tempers were usually good natured and the talk ran along idly with a touch of malice now and then, customarily at the expense of some unhappy youngster trying to measure up to the stature and the manners of the adults. Sometimes old antagonisms came to life in the good-natured jibing and war was declared. George Adcock, a hot-tempered, wiry little gamecock of a man, middle-aged but still belligerent, flew into action one Saturday night against a taller, heavier, and much younger man. There was a brief flurry of blows before the bysitters intervened in the interest of peace, and no decision was rendered, but the younger man sported a black eye for several days as a reminder that there was life in an old dog yet.

With its Rabelaisian overtones, this hot-stove forum was the social page of Tylerville, vastly more lively and human than the social notes in today's newspapers. Those Saturday evenings must have been a drain on the cracker barrel and the wheel of mild American cheese, but they pleased the customers and brought a few cash sales. The aroma of cheese, stale tobacco smoke, and a whiff of harness oil, plus the heavy pungency of an overheated stove is not to be forgotten. To catch it again would bring back the place and the people and the idle talk in spite of the years between. The talkers are long since silent and the life they expressed is buried beyond hope of resurrection in a few dim memories.

CHAPTER III

Rooted In The Soil

I WAS the sixth and last child and I could boast that I was the only one born on our own land, although the inevitable mortgage was to linger about for several years to haunt Father's dreams and absorb most of the cash that came our way. Money, real money, was for the holder of the mortgage and the tax collector; small fry counted their fortunes in pennies.

There is a story of a New York banker that belongs to this period. He was looking over the farm lands in eastern Nebraska and on Sunday he followed his denominational bent and attended the service in a struggling Presbyterian church of the region. When the plate came around he dropped in a twenty-dollar gold piece. It was a big day for the little church. In his blessing over the results the minister called the Lord's attention to the unexpected harvest, much to the embarrassment of the visitor. Money might grow on trees in New York, but not in treeless Nebraska.

My own first taste of capital was the result of a winter's work as janitor of the country school, carrying coal, emptying ashes, starting fires, and sweeping out through the long, cold winter and the raw, muddy spring. My wage was two large silver dollars—the largest I ever saw, paid by the young teacher out of her own small salary. That was the most money I ever received. I was ten years old and I clutched the two coins in a grimy hand and kept the hand in a pants pocket all the way home. Allowances for children were unheard of and a hint that we should be paid for the odd jobs of fetching and carrying that we did around the farm would have been dealt with as economic heresy and filial treason. Didn't the farm give us our keep, our clothing, and the beginnings of an education? The logic of that statement was unbreakable, and it still is. We learned early that the family on the farm was an economic unit and the only one that counted for us.

Since I was the youngest it was assumed that I was of course being spoiled. Older brothers and sisters showed no reluctance in reminding me of their own hard work and self-denial, "when I was your age." I might reject the implication as contrary to the facts of life as I was encountering them, but the assumption stood. It is still my fixed impression that I was saddled with all the dull, dirty jobs that were within my strength, and blamed for most of the things that went wrong. On the latter point my defense was often shaky. The youngest is also the butt of practical jokes of the sort supposed to be amusing to everyone but the victim. I have no recollection of being sent for a left-handed pitchfork. That was reserved for city boys foolishly anxious to be helpful. Almost by the time he learned to walk the country boy was aware of the ambidexterity of things like pitchforks, axes, hoes, and spades.

Only unscrupulous poets and old men with failing memories are sentimental about the joys of childhood. For me childhood was a period of envying and striving for maturity, the time when I should walk tall and strong among my peers, with a strong arm for insults and indignities. In imagination I won all my battles. Viewed in retrospect the actual score seems to have been zero.

While I yearned to be tall and strong, a hope that was never realized, my fondest dreams were of a future in a quite different environment from the one I knew. I had no desire to win fame as a crack cornhusker, an occupation that I despised from my earliest acquaintance with it. I had no faintest wish to excel in the breaking of mean horses. I rode horses and worked them in the field, but I did not love them. Of course, I dreamed of martial glory and more than once saw myself as a frontier deputy marshal, or even as a desperado—always in the interest of justice for the poor and the oppressed. I heard about Robin Hood early. At one time I planned to be an engineer on a crack train, riding my iron horse through storm and darkness, aloof and imperturbable. That didn't last long. Then I toyed with the idea of baseball, with myself, of course, as the pitcher pulling the game out of the fire in the ninth inning. But I never aspired to be the biggest and best farmer anywhere. The moral of these phantom sketches, if there is one, seems to be that the boy concerned was about normal, except perhaps for a slightly oversize dislike for long hours of hard, dull work. Clearly whatever the future held for him, it would not be on a farm if he could help it.

In my early family memories the oldest of us, Fanny and Fred, my seniors by fourteen and thirteen years respectively, were hardly present as brother and sister except by general repute. I may have been three when Fanny was married to Dan Adcock, grandson of Virginia-born Henry, one of the beehunting brothers from down the Illinois fifty years earlier. I am sure that my sister's wedding was the occasion of my first clearly remembered impression. It was not the ceremony or the attendant mild festivities in our small house that engraved themselves on my mind but a lap, a large, slippery, utterly repellent lap into which I was lifted and from which I wriggled as quickly as possible. Of the owner of the lap not a detail remains to me, nor even a faint sense of gratitude for a friendly interest in me, only the hateful lap, shiny, slippery, and probably black.

Dan should have printed himself on my mind as another and welcome brother. He didn't. Brothers were neither new nor always welcome in my narrow cosmos, and I found Dan merely another perplexing and oppressive adult, if anything, more scornfully superior to small boys than those who already surrounded me. I have already indicated that grownups were a great trial to me. Some of them still are. My early contacts with Dan were as brief and sketchy as I could make them, but short as they were, he seldom failed to put a scornful finger on one or more of my many weaknesses.

There was the time when I fell into a pond of muddy water on a raw March day, pulling a panel of fence with me, and made rapid tracks for home and dry clothing. It was weeks before Dan omitted mention of bathing and bathing suits whenever an opening appeared. This was not a form of cruelty, merely a characteristic attitude in a world where only adults counted and children were generally unimportant for what they were and were valued only for what they might become, perhaps healthier than a present tendency to cushion and thus prolong the state of being a child. I was sensitively concerned about myself, and the hazing was bitter medicine.

Much later I knew Dan better and we found a common ground of respect aund understanding, and perspective places him in a more favorable and truer light. Somewhere in his Virginia ancestry there must have been a woods roamer, one of the breed of Boone and Kenton and George Rogers Clark. It was his fate to be born two generations too late, a wilderness hunter compelled to be an Illinois farmer. His hard common sense made him a lover of horses and guns and dogs.

In physique he was short, stocky and powerful, a pocket giant, resourceful, enduring, and unafraid. He had the woodsman's sense of direction and a feeling for the lay of the land. In strange country he could be counted on to find his way as unerringly as though he were living in the day of the long rifle and the coonskin cap. Part of his secret was the fact that he had no fear of being lost, no faintest tendency to panic helplessness. A West Virginia mountaineer, asked if he had ever been lost, put it neatly: "No,I ain't never been lost. Of course, there's been times when I didn't know where I was for two three days, but I ain't never been lost." Dan would have understood that nice distinction.

I was perhaps six or seven when Fred left home, after a few years as a hired man in the neighborhood. Three nearly grown sons were more than the work of an eighty-acre farm demanded, and before he was sixteen he was earning his wage for a near neighbor, another Adcock with more land than sons. Fred's star led him West, that land of hope and high adventure that drew so many boys away from the plodding pace of Illinois furrows, and I knew this brother chiefly through infrequent and uninforming letters. First he was a rider with a cattle outfit in the "short grass" country west of Dodge City out beyond the settler and the barbed wire. That job was a short one and he progressed to a clerkship in Dodge itself. The trail herds were still coming up through the Panhandle and shipping from Dodge City, and it was a lively town after the cattle were loaded and the crew paid off.

The longhorns, descended from the cattle that stampedes and Indians had taken away from the Spaniards, were still to be found in Texas and carloads of them rolled through Galesburg, our market town, bound for the Chicago stockyards, but Herefords were already beginning to push them off the range along with the buffalo and the wild Comanches. I never saw the Old West, but I heard echoes of it from men who were there. Men like my brother never wasted time on "two-gun" literature. It bore too little resemblance to that which they had known. What they remembered was long hours of hard work for small pay. Gunplay was not a popular pastime, and Fred had a supreme contempt for Billy the Kid and his kind. Wild West killings, when they happened, he observed to me long after, were at an extreme range of ten feet, the average width of frontier barrooms, and generally at a target that was facing the other way.

Once, he admitted, he carried a gun for a week when friends had warned him that a shady character in Dodge had been making war talk. Then his sense of humor, plus a knowledge of his own lack of skill in that form of sport, led him to throw his revolver into his trunk and leave it there. His nerve was beyond question. Years later he found himself sheriff in Pueblo, a tough town to be sure, but with the toughness of steel workers by then. The days of the range and the trail were past. In the county jail was a Negro prisoner charged with an unprovoked killing. When a mob hammered on the jail door and demanded its victim, Fred barred the door, stationed his deputies where they could do the most good, and warned the leaders of the mob that the first men in should be sure their life insurance was in order. There were no volunteers for the doubtful honor of the head of the line and there was no lynching. Afterwards I asked him what he thought about that night. He answered drily that he ran over his oath of office in his mind and couldn't find any "excepts" or "unlesses." It was men like that, and not the heroes of pulp and screen, who opened the West and kept it open.

The departure of Fanny and Fred reduced the pressure on our small house at least a little below the bursting point, although there were still six of us to be housed in exceedingly narrow quarters. This was the house that had been standing there when Father bought his original eighty, a smallish living room with a bed in which my parents slept, plus a cot in a corner which was my couch; two small bedrooms overcrowded with double beds, and a leanto kitchen, which of course was also the dining room. My cot had an extension that could be pulled out to make room for a bedfellow in case of need. It was a type believed to have been developed in the Middle West and was called a "lying-in couch." Tradition said that after the inevitable baby was born, mother and infant occupied it so that mother might direct the young and unskilled help, which was the best that most of them could expect. Such cots are collectors' items now, Illinois antiques.

Our house, in common with all other farmhouses, was hot in summer and cold in winter except for the immediate neighborhood of a hot stove on winter evenings. Bedrooms were unheated and breaking the ice in a pitcher of water left standing overnight was a matter of course. What of it? Illinois weather being what it was, and is, what else could be expected?

Small as the house was, an occasional guest or a wayfarer overtaken by storm or darkness was taken in. Tramps and peddlers were fairly frequent callers, although our house was on a side road and not imposing in appearance. Word got around and doubtless many of our visitors had learned over the grapevine telegraph that here were food and lodging for man or beast. At least they were never turned away, although Mother often writhed at thought of such unsavory specimens between her spotless sheets.

There was one that I remember especially. He was a scissors and knife grinder and his services were always in demand. As he ground he talked, reeling off stanzas of verse or hinting at adventure in strange lands. Later I realized that some of his quotations were from John Keats. How did he happen to know them? Obviously by reading. There were public libraries even then. He is remembered as clean and neat and he was shaven. If he had food or a bed he was careful to thank his hostess and to pay in hard cash for his entertainment. He was always welcome but he came seldom, with his shadowy aura of romance and mystery, chapbook wanderer out of place and time in that Illinois farm country.

There was another, an Irishman with a pack of linen and laces and a glib tongue. He displayed his wares at Jerry Hawkins' blacksmith shop one day and Johnny Lee, an Irish neighbor, was among the onlookers. As the peddler talked, Johnny interposed a question. "Tell me," he said, "are the Irish people as hard customers as the others?" "No," said the peddler. "I'm glad of that," interjected Johnny. The peddler went smoothly on as he adjusted his pack: "Not as hard," he said, "but a dommed sight harder!" Exit Johnny.

When there was need, a hard cot in the leanto kitchen was pressed into service, and for boys three or even four in one bed were none too many. What those narrow bedrooms with a single window each were like on hot nights in an Illinois summer cannot be stated in polite terms, but hot or cold we had no need for sleeping pills. A long day in the harvest field was sedative enough.

On one July night I remember that Phil had the bright idea of cooling off by a dip in the cistern of rainwater below ground near the window. Slipping off his scanty nightshirt, he slid the cover off the cistern and dropped into five feet of water chilled by many days of sub-surface refrigeration, a pioneer deep freeze. It is of record that he came out as quickly as he went in and the experiment was not repeated.

Our heating system was simple, a cookstove in the kitchen and a "heating" stove in the living room. Our fuel came from the timber—we never called it woods—that still occupied nearly half the farm. Many beautiful trees went up farmhouse chimneys in a cold winter. Carrying wood and kindling for household use was one of the jobs that fell to the lot of the small boy as soon as his arms were strong enough.

The sanitary provisions of all farmhouses was the same, the outside privy, roasting hot and noisy with the buzzing of flies in summer and cold beyond words in winter. The simple life was a rigorous one and only the hardier survived. Bathrooms were unknown and running water belonged in streams.

In summer we of the sterner sex knew of ponds and swimming holes that served our purposes of recreation and mild cleanliness. The water in these primitive swimming pools was always muddy and the sanitary effect of the swim was doubtful, but at least we rid ourselves of the dust acquired in the course of a hot day in the harvest field or plowing corn.

Bathing in winter in narrow, crowded quarters was not exciting nor particularly pleasant. I'm sure that my own performance on cold Saturday nights was perfunctory, even under pressure. Water supply presented few problems. Abundant summer rains and winter snows kept ground and cisterns well filled, and a twenty-five foot well was an unusually deep one. If a new well was needed we dug it where we wanted it and the water was there.

One I remember particularly. It was only half a dozen yards from the back kitchen door and less than that from the old well that had played us false. Phil was the digger, Charlie was the top man dumping the buckets of earth, and I was the bored driver of the horse that hoisted the bucket. All was proceeding according to plan when there came a shout from the depths. We hurried to the side and looked down. There, a matter of twenty feet down, we glimpsed the sparkle of running water. Everyone knows that there are no underground rivers, only a "stratum of permeable soil," but there was flowing water down below. We had found the thing that couldn't be there. That was the only possible explanation. There was a frenzied dash to a local blacksmith shop for a hoop of steel large enough to fit inside our well. This was lowered to the man below and a casing of boards set to stop the caving of the almost liquid sand, and we had our well. There was never great depth of water, but it lasted a long time. Then it too conked out.

The universal pump was the old-fashioned wooden variety worked by hand with a simple plunger in the pipe to create the vacuum that brought the water to the surface. In severe cold a simple device drained the water out of the pipe as a precaution against freezing. It didn't always work, but a kettleful of hot water would break the ice jam in the pipe and all was well. "Priming the pump" was a common country phrase and not a controversial political issue.

We knew about dowsing and some of the neighbors believed in it as they believed in the Ten Commandments and the Republican Party, but we called it "witching for water." We Britts didn't hold by dowsing, but I experimented with it to see what would happen and to secure brief release from the endless chores. The technique is simple. All that is required is a fork cut from green hazel, preferably in the dark of the moon. The operator must hold the prongs of the fork firmly in his hands, with his thumbs pointing downward. The position of the thumbs is important. Holding it thus, the dowser walks slowly about in the area under examination. Presently the mystic pull of the underground stream gets in its work and the fork turns slowly until the stem points straight downward and there the water will be found. Usually it was there—and also anywhere else in that well-saturated Illinois soil.

My experiments were highly unscientific in method, but they convinced one person. Me. I concluded that the strained position of the hands on the hazel fork turned the ends of the fork outwards and in response the stem turned down, even when the hazel was gripped so tightly that the bark was loosened. Clearly thls was mighty magic, but the might was physical, a fact of torsion and not a mystery.

When our wells went dry in prolonged drought, we were more fortunate than most in having an emergency supply near at hand. Three or four hundred yards from our house was an unfailing spring which had been boxed in against such a time of need. Bringing the water to the house meant a long carry up a steep hill through the woods with a brimming pail in each hand. Father lightened the task by making a "carrying yoke," fitted to neck and shoulders with clever curves. A heavy cord hung from each end with a hook at the end for the pails. Such yokes are used by Chinese peasants to this day for the same kind of work. Our day leaned heavily on a primitive past and in many ways our modern cultural habits are only skin-deep.

In seasons of drought the watering of stock was one of our tasks, and sometimes an exciting one. Young horses would step quickly and obediently down the hill to the spring, knowing well what waited for them at the bottom. But taking them back to their stalls, full of cold water and high spirits, was something quite otherwise. At such a time leading two or three docile workhorses was a prospect that I viewed with misgivings, and half-broken colts were nothing less than a menace. No desert-dweller prayed for rain more fervently than I.

As the streams died, stock in the pasture were also driven to the blessed spring. I learned to ride early, Indian fashion, bareback, hanging on by knees, heels, the horse's mane, and the grace of God. On a day that I remember, Banty, my favorite mount, and I were pelting on the heels of a band of horses along a road cleared through the underbrush and scrubby second growth. Without reason or warning my charges crashed off the road into the underbrush and we crashed after; that is, Banty did. I did an improvised swan dive over her withers and landed on hands and knees half in front of her. Thanks to Banty's quick feet the worst I had to show for it was a graze on a leg, not enough to excite much sympathy at home when I exhibited my wound. Handling horses was no work for a dreamer.

CHAPTER IV

The Cat That Figured Things Out

THE EIGHTIES were hard years for farmers. Prices for farm products were low, sometimes twelve or fifteen cents a bushel for corn, three dollars a hundredweight or less for hogs. Industry was booming and prices were high for goods the farmer must buy. There was discontent in the air, and the farmer was beginning to grumble out loud. Coming or going, he was on the losing end of every transaction. But unending work and rigid economy would bring results. There was no money for luxuries or even the simplest pleasures; the farm took it all, but the farm paid dividends and the value of the land was increasing. However gloomy the news from the Chicago Board of Trade, we ate well and slept well through the zero winters.

I was approaching my tenth year when there was positive evidence of improvement in our balance sheet. The strongest proof was the purchase of the "Prushaver eighty" adjoining ours. The plowland in this addition was rougher and less fertile than our own, but the pasture land was welcome, watered as it was by a small creek, the Big Branch, that flowed through the middle of it. Now we had achieved the ideal family farm of that day, a quarter of a section, large enough to justify a working force of three adults with the small-scale machinery of that time.

Soon after its purchase the Prushaver farm was the scene of one of my more exciting adventures. Wolf tracks were seen in the snow occasionally, to be identified by the greater length of their middle toes. These were the gray timber wolves, smaller than the giants of the North, but big and fierce enough to handle most

31

farm dogs. Pigs, sheep, and young calves were favored items on the wolf menu, and a night or two before my adventure one had paid a call on the Trepening sheep pasture, leaving two of the "woolies" with their throats neatly cut. The clean slash with which the murder was accomplished exonerated the dogs of the neighborhood. Another incriminating circumstance was the evidence that the marauder had slipped between the rails of the fence around the pasture instead of going over the top dog fashion.

The crowning offense was that the bodies of the dead sheep were lying only two or three hundred yards from the kennel where Dan Adcock's hounds were sleeping the sleep of the virtuous. The dogs did their belated best early the next morning to follow the trail but lost it at the Big Branch where the crafty killer had trotted up or downstream far enough to baffle them.

One of our sows had elected to choose a strip of underbrush on the far side of the new farm as a lying-in hospital. Part of my duties was to take corn to her late in the afternoon each day, and in due course I set forth accompanied by my constant companion Dash, reputed to have a touch of greyhound in his confused family tree and a mighty hunter before the Lord when the game was rabbits. That wolf was very much in my mind after the affair in the Terpening pasture, but Mrs. Pig was hungry and the wolf had probably put miles behind him by that time.

The corn had been delivered and I was turning back when Dash burst into vigorous cry not far away. My instinctive thought was of a provoking squirrel safe on a high limb and I whistled Dash to come along and stop his nonsense. That was once when my whistle brought prompt obedience. There was a swift rustling in the leaves and my dog burst into view twenty feet away, with a large and businesslike wolf on his heels. My response was prompt and speedy. Dash had a running start and was doing his best, but it is my recollection that I passed him in less than a hundred yards. At the top of the hill on the other side of the Big Branch, boy and dog stopped for breath and a look back. There on the top of another low hill was my wolf, sitting on his haunches watching us out of sight. Apparently all he wanted was to see the last of us.

About the time that we doubled the size of our farm we built a new house, a two-story mansion no less. The new house boasted a large kitchen with a pantry, a good-sized living room, and my parents' bedroom on the ground floor, to say nothing of front and back porches. On the second floor were three rooms, the largest of which with two double beds became the "boys' room." Now I was promoted from the humble cot of my beginnings to a share in a big room and a place in a double bed. In all other respects I was still "the kid," occupying the lowest level of unskilled labor.

Farmhouses were built without benefit of architect or reference to a particular style or period. Such plans as existed were principally in the head of the local carpenter who bossed the job. Ours was named Perkins and he came from Alexis, all of six miles away. I have no further information about him, except his son who worked on the job was married soon after. When she heard that, Mother remarked darkly that she knew something was wrong with him. Love apparently.

A model of our house could have been made easily with a set of child's building blocks, but it was roomy and comfortable without dormers, turrets, or scrollsaw ornamentation, which were unpleasantly common on dwellings of that time. Prime consideration was enough interior space to suit family needs, and if the house was leakproof through rain and snow and windproof for anything short of a cyclone, all hands were satisfied. Houses were painted white, window blinds green. Barns were always painted red and as the color weathered some of the old barns were beautiful. If a barn was in sight from the road it usually had the year of construction painted on it in large white numerals. Our new house cost nearly a thousand dollars and it was still a good investment when it burned down nearly thirty years later. The man hours of labor embodied in that thousand dollars would cost ten or twenty times that amount today.

With the building of a new home the little old one became a stable for horses, and the leanto kitchen the family smokehouse. It was the latter structure that gave me the opportunity to watch what I still regard as a demonstration of the power of reason in animals, a quality generally regarded as the special property of some human beings. The actor in this case was the farm cat, a well-fed mongrel called Tom because that was the kind of cat he was. We always had at least one cat and one dog as working members of the family and took them for granted as subordinate cogs in the farm machine. Animal psychology was unknown to us even as a term. We knew only that cats were cats and dogs were dogs and both were expected to behave as such.

Tom's regular business was with the mice and rats that were always with us. He was skillful in taking care of himself and never failed to appear at the kitchen door at suppertime. On winter evenings he was seldom far from the kitchen stove and made bitter comment when admission was delayed. Summer and winter he was well informed on the milking schedule and was generally in the neighborhood of the door of the cowshed where the pails of fresh milk were kept on a high shelf until all the cows were stripped. To Tom there was no such thing as an inaccessible shelf if there was milk on it, and he had found a circuitous route by which he could reach the shelf from above. I suppose he worked it out himself, but if I thought about it at all, it was as a typical cat trick.

Father's temper was on the explosive side, especially where petty lawbreaking was concerned, and the results of Tom's approach to the forbidden shelf could be both seen and heard, first a shout of rage from Father, then a dark gray streak along the path from cowshed to kitchen door. When the streak rounded the henhouse halfway to the goal, it slowed to a large gray cat sauntering sedately along, smugly licking his chops. All he needed to complete his imitation of a satisfied hired hand leaving the table of his own accord was a toothpick in the corner of his mouth. Along with his observations of the route to the milk shelf, he had also noted the route of effective retreat, a point often overlooked in military tactics. Father's affair with Tom was an almost daily occurrence, but none of us had seen anything more than a mildly amusing episode and further proof that a cat was a cat. Some cats were obviously smarter than others, and Tom might be in a feline IQ bracket a little above average. That was all.

The smokehouse incident was something else. The door that guarded the smoking hams and sides of bacon was closed by a simple latch operated by pressing down with a thumb on a projection provided for that purpose. As a lock it was a short step ahead of the primitive wooden affair with a string run through a hole in the door. We knew about those, too. "The latch string is always out" was a familiar saying then. Old latches of the smokehouse variety are collectors' items in these Yale & Towne days, but they were common seventy years ago; any crossroads blacksmith could hammer one out for you. These simple details are essential to an understanding of the laboratory in which Tom staged his demonstration. That latch was a primitive device, if you please, but using it was not a natural part of a cat's way of life.

Complaints began to accumulate that the door had been found open at a time when smoking was in progress, evidence of a misdemeanor at least. Being the youngest I was suspect by status as well as by reputation. It was assumed that if there was carelessness about, no one was so likely to be the guilty party as the kid, part of the hard lot of being the youngest. Circumstance and assumption combined to point an accusing finger at me. Just when my case seemed hopeless pure luck came to my rescue, luck and the unconquerable Tom.

As I came slowly around the corner of the house one happy day I saw the feline experiment reach its successful climax. Tom was crouched at the door looking up at the latch, clearly absorbed in important calculations, quite unaware that a witness had arrived. He crouched, he jumped, with one forepaw he reached for the handgrip below the thumb-latch, seeking to hold himself a moment in position, and with the other paw he struck down at the latch. Three times he tried and missed, devoted an interval to further calculation, and tried again. Clearly this was no new experience for him. Finally he scored a bull's-eye on the latch, his weight against the door, swung it back, and Tom was in. So help me, I saw it happen.

Was his success proof of a reasoning process beyond anything usually ascribed to the lower animals? I don't know; that's for animal psychologists, to whom I make free gift of this report.

But if Tom didn't open that door as a result of observation, deduction, and conclusion, how did he do it? By pure chance? Not Tom. He wasn't that kind of a cat. All his risks were calculated.

The picture of Tom absorbed in his task, matching his wits against the obstructions that civilization had set in the way of his legitimate activities, has become the cornerstone of my firm belief that cats are more intelligent than any other of our domestic animals. The horse, for all the praise that is heaped on him, is a creature of habit, occasionally interrupted by eccentric fears. I have seen staid old workhorses who would plod wearily from end to end of a long field through a long day and then on the way back to the barn snort and jump out from under the rider at the sight of a leaf blowing across the road. Is that proof of horse sense?

Everybody says that the dog is man's best friend, but I wonder. Our dogs, and we always had at least one, were slaves fawning on the master class, trading independence willingly for a bone and a place to sleep on cold nights, usually in the haymow. They would join enthusiastically in pursuits for which they were naturally fitted, such as chasing rabbits or driving stock, and with care they could be made efficient in either of these fields. Yes, I know that sheep dogs are good at handling sheep. I've seen them do it, but I do not recall a dog who ever discovered that a squirrel is not a rabbit and that a dog cannot climb a tree. I would hesitate to guess how many times I have been a witness of the futile comedy of a well-meaning Dash or Ring standing on his hindlegs against a tree doing his ludicrous best to climb up and put an end to the insulting comments of a squirrel.

That sort of performance has gone on since dogs and squirrels first appeared on earth, and there is no record of a single dog realizing that the tree dweller was making a fool of him. A cat that failed to figure out a simple thing like that would long since have been ostracized by his fellow cats as feeble-minded. Although he was probably the earliest of the so-called dumb animals to be exposed to the blandishments of human society, he alone has made his bargain with humanity on terms set and largely administered by himself. The price he pays is the minimum, chiefly bland ac-

ceptance of a congenial diet and a comfortable pl
The mice and gophers—and songbirds—that he dra
for his own use. He takes the human race in his str
sary he can get along without it.

Chapter V

White Oak And Black Hickory

I
N SPITE of the bland assertion of school geographies that
Illinois is a prairie state, one of my early impressions of our
environment was of trees. They were all about us, shutting us in
from sight of open fields except in the leafless days of winter.
Our farm was cut and burned and grubbed out of the thick
timber and underbrush with infinite, backbreaking labor. This
battle with nature was still in progress when I arrived at consciousness. The new eighty which we had acquired had stretches
of scrub growth and heavy brush that must be turned into plowland or pasture. My part in this painful process was slight, mostly
piling and burning the slashings. Sometimes this was interesting,
much more so than trying to play a man's part at one end of a
crosscut saw. The most blighting comment that could come from
the other end of the saw was: "I don't mind yer ridin' the saw, but
stop draggin' yer feet."

One winter Phil and Charlie took on the job of clearing
a corner of heavy growth for Dan, and I was drafted on Saturdays
and holidays as brush burner. This had enough resemblance to
pioneering to stimulate the imagination to temporary forgetful-
ness of the drudgery. To add to the illusion the place was too far
from home to permit easy return for midday dinner and we lunched
briefly from a big tin pail. On such days I learned to my surprise
that fat meat, previously viewed with acute distaste, could be delicious, especially when the sandwich containing it was toasted at
the end of a sharp stick over the hot coals of a brush fire. Solid fat
was even better than frozen apple pie. The smell of burning wood

and the tang of smoke in the winter air added mightily to the illusion of pioneering.

Grubbing stumps was plain hard work without illusions. We heard of stump pulling machines that lightened the labor, but such devices were for the monied aristocrats of farming. We took the hard way. The tools were axe and grub hoe, a narrow, long-bladed tool with a straight handle. Mattock is the modern term, I believe. The technique of grubbing was simple; clear away the earth around the roots with the hoe and cut the roots below the level of the plow, and keep at it until the stump was out. The trees that gave us the most trouble were the hickories. These had sturdy taproots straight down from the center of the stump, underground continuations of the trunk of the tree. The grubber worked on his knees in an awkward, cramped position, half in the hole of his own digging, cutting the stubborn root with little room to swing the axe or to see the target. An unkind neighbor once watched me trying for the root with indifferent success. Then he summed up his observations tersely: "You're the first fellow I ever saw that could hit three times and land in four different places." Clearly I was not meant to be a pioneer.

We heard that in early days landlookers judged the quality of soil by the character of tree growth. There were two kinds of soil, white oak and black oak, the former easily plowed, fertile, and absorbing freely the warmth of the early spring sun, the latter sour, cold, and unfriendly. Our farm had both white oak and black, putting us somewhere in between. I do not vouch for the accuracy of these categories, but it was evidently a common belief. At least the theory illustrates the part that trees played in the early pattern of living, even in a land predominantly level and treeless. Trees gave us firewood and fencing, cordwood for sale or barter, and saw logs for turning into boards at a local sawmill.

Soon after taking root in a fixed place, thereby acquiring status and credit, Father established amicable relations with a shoemaker in Galesburg and until I lost daily touch with family fortunes, the price of a pair of boots made to his measure was a cord of black hickory. As I grew older I viewed this bit of primitive barter as somehow humiliating, but primitive or not, I've never been able to afford shoes made to order or of such good leather.

Incidentally, the small-town shoemaker of the old breed has long since disappeared, along with the locksmith, the gunsmith and the harnessmaker. Now we dance to the tune called by the United Shoe Machinery Co., the assembly line, the chain store, and the servurself market. No doubt the change was inevitable, but some of the color has gone out of country towns with the passing of these gifted artisans and their salty wisdom.

Scattered through the timber about us were varieties of trees that have almost ceased to exist in that part of Illinois. I have mentioned hickory. The black hickory was the American tree par excellence in the Midwest as the chestnut was in the East. It grew straight and tall, with long stretches of the trunk clear of branches and knots, not unlike the chestnut in appearance. Among the hickory's many virtues its greatest were its strength and its resilience. The Indians knew it well and used it for their bows. Outside of hickory country they were forced back on other woods, such as the osage, once widely used as hedges where material for fences was lacking, or Oregon yew.

The pioneers found hickory perfect for axe helves and the running gear of wagons and carriages. The American axe in the hands of a real woodsman was a precision tool. The head of the single-bitted (bladed) type was cleverly shaped to give it maximum cutting efficiency with a minimum of weight. The helve was curved and perfectly suited to its function. Wielded by a woodsman it made the standard day's work a cord of hickory, cut, split, and piled. (For the benefit of a more sophisticated and less informed generation, a cord is four feet high, four feet wide, and eight feet long.)

A mark of the expert was his swing, deceptively slow and easy, until one noted the speed with which the axe bit into the wood, vastly different from the ragged gnawing of the tyro. The old characterization of the artist in this ancient craft was to say that you could write a letter on the face of his cut. Hickory cut by such men made the early Studebaker wagons the standard of excellence among us and carried the fame of the high-wheeled sulky and trotting horse around the world. A good wood, hickory; too bad there's so little of it left.

Hickory nuts deserve a chapter of their own. Their shells were hard to crack, and it was harder still to extract the kernel from the convoluted and involuted interior, but once out the meat had a flavor and a sweetness all its own, superior in my memory to the pecan of the South or the famed chestnut of the East. Compared with the hickory nut the English walnut of commerce is without character or distinction. The nuts of the black hickory must not be confused with those of the white hickory, poor cousin of the black. These were thin-shelled and bitter, pig nuts we called them, and only pigs and chipmunks ate them willingly. Squirrels turned up their noses at them if real nuts were to be had.

Time was when black hickory trees were dotted through the timber around us, with here and there a towering specimen of the "big" variety strayed up from the Mississippi bottoms. The big nuts were about the size of English walnuts and better in taste, but not up to the level of the smaller kind. Farm cooks sprinkled hickory nuts through cake in place of the rare and expensive raisin, and they were often in homemade candy. My own version of gastronomic luxury was hickory nuts and a ripe apple, Snow preferred, eaten together. If Olympus overlooked this delicate combination the high gods missed a bet. At least that was the way it seemed to me long ago.

When the first frosts came was the time to gather the nuts from the ground, where they had fallen through the night, and shake down those that still clung to the branches. Old men who have known those late October afternoons with a nip in the air in spite of the golden sunshine can feel again the cool wind blowing in spite of the years and miles between and hear the rustle of the dead leaves through which they searched for hickory nuts. We dried them in the sun to make sure of the final touch of ripeness and then stored them against the long winter evenings. The proper place for cracking them was on the edge of a flatiron held between the knees—never on the polished face of the iron if you valued your life.

Tapped gently but firmly with a hammer they would sometimes break neatly into halves, but not often. However small the fractions they were always good. Cracking hickory nuts or walnuts was no job for a young man in a hurry.

There were other nut trees in our Illinois timber, black walnuts and butternuts for example. Of course there were hazel nuts, bushels of them, but those are from bushes, not trees. We rated hazel nuts rather low in our scale of desirability, although their resemblance to the English filbert gave them some sentimental title to consideration. The American walnut is a handsome tree, tall and straight, and the rich darkness of the wood rivals mahogany. Properly sawed and matched walnut boards present a grain design that is almost too flamboyant. The paneling in the presidential office of the Mormon church in Salt Lake City shows the walnut butterfly pattern at its showiest. Seasoned walnut demands sharp tools and careful handling. Early settlers sometimes chose it for window and door trim and similar uses. I know at least two old houses still standing where not only the trim but stair rail and doors recall a day before the lumber yard and the mill had succeeded in gearing our tastes to the speed of the bandsaw and power-driven lathes and planes.

Black walnuts are definitely edible, although the flavor is too pronounced for delicate palates. The outer casing of the nut produces a dark brown dye, as the picker's fingers will testify, akin to the color that northern troops saw on Confederate uniforms, when they had time to look closely. There were two of these beautiful trees in our dooryard, as the squirrels of the neighborhood well knew. We had a few butternuts, the nuts easier to crack and with a milder flavor than the walnut. I'm sure that I could still find a few of all these trees if I were to wander along ways that I once walked, but it would be like pulling the vines and weeds away from crumbling headstones in old, long neglected graveyards.

I have spoken of oaks, white and black. The white was the aristocrat. It had the sweet, mealy acorns that the squirrels collected and I have a dim recollection that the Indians, and the white pioneers after them, pounded these acorns to a coarse meal and mixed it with ground corn for bread. Give a white oak fifty years of growth, and it would show you a massive trunk and a great spread of branches, both trunk and branches at their best when there were no close neighbors, sturdy individualists as they were. Oak boards, two inches thick, made the planking for our country bridges and the beams for houses and barns.

Hewing was no job for the weak or the slovenly. A broadaxe, which was favored over the adz in our parts, was correctly named. The cutting edge was about twice the length of the ordinary chopping axe and the weight also was nearly double, making it a clumsy article in the hands of a tyro. The log was first "scored" with an ordinary axe, slanting the cuts to about the depth required. Then came the man with the broadaxe to cut off the chips that the scoring had begun. The finished beam must be of even diameter in cross section from end to end of the log, with smooth surfaces and no splinters or deep axe marks. The axemen who could do this died long ago. Pioneering was a hard schooling in homely, necessary arts.

A local name for the white oak was post oak. It split easily and smoothly and was highly resistant to the attacks of insects and to dampness. Those qualities made the wood ideal for the board fences we built around house yards and barn lots. Once a year the white oak was a calendar for farmers. Corn planting time had come when the leaves on the oaks were as large as squirrels' ears. This was a heritage from Indian lore passed down to the early settlers.

Black oak was limited in its usefulness. It was firewood of course, but any wood will burn if it is well seasoned and dry. Heat-producing qualities depend on speed of combustion. The chief service of black oak for us was its provision of the stake and rider fences, "worm fences" in some places because of their zigzag construction, which enclosed our fields before the modern barbarism of barbed wire appeared to tear and scar young horses who tried to jump it. It must have been black oak that young Lincoln split down there in Sangamon County. I too have helped split rails, but not with such startling effect. It may have been something else that started young Abraham on his way.

The building or repairing of rail fences was one of the farm tasks reserved for slack times in the fields. There were no periods of idleness. The standard length of a fence rail was ten feet and it must be straight and with few knots. The young man who could clear a rail in a standing jump was entitled to honorable mention. In building, the fence rails were overlapped at the corners much as a child might overlap match sticks, and successive lengths of fence were at an angle to each other to insure stability. To provide the proper fence, "horse high, hog tight, and bull strong," stakes were set at the corners crossing each other above the top. In the crotch thus formed, another rail, the "rider," was laid to discourage horses afflicted with a wanderlust. Rail fences were picturesque, but their making called for the slaughter of many trees and what seemed endless hours of hard labor, and their corners harbored a rank growth of weeds and briars. When the briars were wild blackberries a useful by-product was assured.

Material for fences was always a problem for the farmer, especially as the tide carried him westward. Early New Englanders built stone walls with infinite labor. Hard as the work was, it served a double purpose. The walls not only enclosed the fields, but they also got the stones off the ground and gave the plows a chance. But the homesteaders of the plains had neither stones nor trees. What to do? Ditches were tried and high ridges of earth, probably giving rise to the homely phrase, "ugly as a mud fence." Neither ditch nor ridge was effective, especially in a dry country.

The osage, growing wild in southern Kansas and eastern Oklahoma, seemed an answer to the farmer's prayer. It grew close and high and was armed with sharp thorns that even cattle and hogs soon learned to respect. The seeds were contained in a large, yellowish, orange-like fruit about the size of a baseball and it grew fast even in dry country, but there were marked disadvantages. Unless it was trimmed at least every two years it got out of hand and threw its shade over a wide belt, stunting the crops where the shadow lay. In spite of this fault the use of the osage hedge spread widely, and prairie farms in Illinois planted miles and miles of it. Jonathan W. Turner from Jacksonville acquired considerable local fame by electing himself the apostle of hedge planting, bearing the gospel through the state. J. F. Glidden's barbed wire, first produced in 1874, put an end to all the argument and incidentally pulled the farmer a little more intimately into our growing industrial economy. No one could have imagined the sinister role that would be played by barbed wire in France in the first World War when great armies burrowed underground and filled the No-Man's land between the trenches with wire entanglements, but it did simplify fencing.

Our tree growth included a few elms, more picturesque than useful in the farm economy. The wood was tough and hard to split, with stubborn splinters resisting to the last, quite different from the smooth, easy cleavage of white oak and hickory. Indians sometimes contrived passable bows from young elm, but for our needs boards sawed from it were likely to warp and it was unpopular as firewood because of the length of time required for its seasoning.

Wild cherry should not be ignored. We had many of them, tall trees with long straight trunks, eighteen inches or more at the butt. Father once had a big money idea. We would cut our larger cherries, have them sawed, and sell the boards at a fancy price to some furniture maker who would of course jump at the chance of picking up a few loads of this hardwood, with its high color, its beautiful grain, and its smooth polished surface. Unfortunately, after the logs had been sawed we were unable to find a furniture maker near enough to do the jumping. As far as we were concerned Grand Rapids might as well have been in Timbuctoo, and the family bonanza turned out to be only another pile of lumber. Perhaps something had been overlooked in the mousetrap story. There is a local market now, but, alas, there are no such trees any more.

Another beautiful and useful tree of which there were a few groves in our neighborhood was the hard maple, although ours was not really a maple country. I saw one group of sugar trees flourish and die in George Sallee's timber a short half mile from our house. My earliest recollection of it is of the sugar camp there in early spring. It was a small-scale affair, but I am prepared to make reasonable affidavit that the syrup and sugar it produced were as good as Vermont's and a long sight better than the commercial brands, whose labels make grudging confession to a dalliance with corn syrup. A brother took me to the camp one night and I had the thrill of tasting the syrup in its final boiling, dipped from the pan and cooled on a snowbank lingering outside the door.

A year or two later I saw the peripatetic sawmill that had moved in doing its murderous work of converting living beauty into lifeless boards. Boards could be sold. Beauty could only be enjoyed. The hillside where the maples grew, sloping down to a little stream, now boasts a few scrubby trees with neither market value nor beauty and straggling tangles of underbrush. The stream is dry now except in time of heavy rain or melting snow.

There on a small scale was the unlovely side of the development—and waste—of our resources of which we are so proud. One hears much talk of reforestation, but sees far too little of it. The farmer's trees built his fences, his barns, and his houses, and kept him warm on winter nights, but he left his heirs to shift for themselves. There were a few exceptions. Years later a nephew showed me with pride a little clump of virgin oak that by some chance had escaped the axe and the saw. I don't know how good a farmer he was, but I remember that day with gratitude.

Chapter VI

The Little Red School House

SCHOOL days are the golden days. At least that's what everybody says. And the purest gold were those days in the little one-room country school, now embalmed in tradition. "Reading and writing and 'rithmetic/Taught to the tune of a hickory stick." Everybody praises it, but nobody tells what it was like, really. I began my long search for an education in such a school, about 1880 it was.

I heard of school first as a distant place to which brothers and sisters disappeared often and for long hours. What they did there had some mysterious relation to things called letters and figures, about which I was beginning to be curious. I must have made an experimental visit there with them, near the age of five at a guess. I recall only being told afterwards that I had disgraced the family by going to sleep and falling off a much too high seat. That was not the last time I went to sleep in school, but I remember no other similar feat of falling from the seat and from grace at the same time.

Was that perhaps merely my first day of regular attendance? I haven't a ghost of an idea. The mile and a half over a hilly, wooded road was a long trek for five-year old legs, but we started young in those days and school buses were sixty years away. I was to know that road well in the next ten years. There was the high bridge where a horse had gone through the shaky railing and the turn in the road where I'd surprised a skunk digging in a rotten log and bombarded him with sticks from a safe distance. (That is, I thought it was safe. It wasn't.) There was a swampy

bit where the cowslips bloomed in early spring. When we saw
them we knew it was almost time to go barefoot. (There are few
sensations in life to compare with the feel of soft moist earth
under your bare feet. You're sure that you could run forever,
your feet are so light and free.) The big white oak with the huge
limb that thrust out at a right angle ten feet above the ground must
not be overlooked. That was where the panther crouched waiting
for a small boy to come along. I saw him there many times, although
of course there wasn't any panther. By that time I was reading
adventure stories in *The Youth's Companion*, and my imagination
was working overtime.

About the time I started, a tentative attempt was made to
open another school by cutting a slice off each of two adjoining
districts. The new school was in a spare room of a rambling old
farmhouse a quarter of a mile away from where we lived. It didn't
last long, but it pleased me while it lasted. Our schools were happy-
go-lucky affairs, so far as administrative controls went. If enough
families decided to start a school of their own, no one was likely
to interfere, so long as they paid their bills. As for district boundaries, the good old rule of common consent sufficed.

Unfortunately for me the experiment failed to justify itself
and after a single term I was back on the long trail. By and large
I conclude that country school was the first real bulge in the peri-
meter of my consciousness, and continued to play a major role in
my life until I was sixteen and facing the need of preparing for
college. It is there that many of the most vivid memories of my
childhood center.

We knew our school as Science Hall, but officially it was
District Four in Kelly Township. The schoolhouse still stands
where it was built ninety years ago, a plain rectangular building
with a narrow entry where coats and overshoes were deposited.
At the front end of the schoolroom, between the two doors through
which the children came, was the teacher's desk, a table with a
sloping top, standing on a low platform to add to the sense of
superior command. Desks were in three rows facing the teacher,
plain wooden affairs, each one accommodating two small bodies.

Each seat was attached to the front of the desk behind it at right angles to it, making no concessions to the curves or comforts of the human spine. All seats were at the same height from the floor, regardless of the age or height of the occupant. The designers of these desks were clearly Spartan by nature, if not by blood.

In an open space about ten feet square in front of the teacher's dais was the heating plant, a cast-iron, potbellied temperamental stove burning quantities of soft coal. When properly banked down with fine coal, enough gas might accumulate to touch off a miniature explosion, filling the room with smoke and making a welcome break in the tiresome routine of education. There were three windows on a side and none at the back, which was given over entirely to a blackboard for the demonstration of our uncertain skills in arithmetic and the parsing of sentences in the study of grammar. I became moderately skillful in putting together the crude diagrams by which we indicated the relations of subject, object, predicate, and modifiers, but the essence of grammar remained a mystery to me until I encountered first-year Latin in preparatory school, at least one good reason for the study of Latin.

In general that schoolroom was a barren, cheerless place, with no attempts at decoration except an occasional bunch of wildflowers on the desk of a popular woman teacher in the spring. School budgets had no room for pictures or books, and wall maps were few and little used. Besides, decorations might distract the attention of the children from their books, and it was in books, as everyone knew, that education was to be found. Life was not only real and earnest, but it was also tough, and school was part of our apprenticeship. The logic of this was unanswerable.

The builders of our school had been wiser than they knew. On one side was wooded pasture land and on the other open prairie, by my time under cultivation. The line where prairie and woodland met was as sharply marked as timber line on high mountains. The environment had varied possibilities for us. There were hills for coasting in the winter and woods and underbrush criss-crossed with rabbit tracks to whet the hunting appetite. Open stretches of pasture or stubble gave room for our version of baseball. To prove that we were on the line between woodland and prairie, a big oak tree adorned one corner of the yard and somewhere among its upper branches my initials may still be found carved in the trunk as proof of climbing prowess that was once mine. Two wild crabapple trees stood nearby, providing occasional ammunition for playground battles, at considerable hazard to schoolhouse windows. One of the small hard apples stuck on the pointed end of a limber hazel switch had amazing range combined with high velocity.

Science Hall was of the old breed of "little red schoolhouse," long remembered and highly praised. It had its faults and its virtues. It was there and it was open to all on equal terms. For country children it was all there was; the alternative was nothing at all. At this distance praise and blame are alike idle. These schools were outposts in the long battle against ignorance and illiteracy. If they won few major battles, they held their own in a lot of forgotten skirmishes and cleared the way for larger engagements.

Organization and administration were simple, and teaching methods were as individual teachers chose, usually a stumbling repetition of the textbook. When country superintendents were good, which was far from always, they struggled to bring order and pattern out of democratic chaos, mainly by counsel and exhortation, but control was largely in the hands of the three directors elected by the voters of the district. They hired the teachers, usually local products of the school they were to teach, or another one very like it. Salaries were low, twenty dollars a month or less for women, more for men, preferred for the winter term when the "big boys" came. No other attempt was made to justify the sex differential in the pay scale. Women were often the better teachers, more devoted and concerned with their pupils, but men were worth more than women without regard to the quality of the work done, and that was all there was to it. As one local director put it, "A woman just ain't worth thirty dollars a month."

When I referred to the big boys in the winter term I meant just that. There was Johnny Mahoney, eighteen or nineteen years old, fully grown and powerful, still in the lower grades if there had been grades, a hundred and seventy-five pounds of Irish good humor. Johnny habitually smoked a big pipe in the school yard at recess and observed our childish games with tolerant amusement. When my brother Charlie and Maurice Bride, both well on in their teens, goaded each other from a state of tacit animosity to open combat, Molly and the other girls appealed to Johnny to "make them quit." He smiled his broad smile around his pipe stem and kept his hands comfortably in his pockets. "Let 'em fight it out," he said. "Do 'em good." What was a fight more or less to an Irishman? Fortunately for all concerned, the teacher for that term went home for lunch. It was the standing rule with men teachers that a fight called for a sound thrashing for both contestants, regardless of cause or outcome. Evidently there was no such thing as a just war. In this case, both fighters were bigger and stronger than the teacher and they knew it. Probably the teacher knew it too.

Most of us, too small to make a thrashing embarrassing to anyone but ourselves, were forced to rely on a tacit code for such affairs of honor. Playground differences demanding violent settlement were to be dealt with on the outside, preferably on the way home. Meanwhile no hint was to be given that could reach the ears of the teacher or the girls, some of whom were quite capable of telling on us in the interest of peace. There was the case of Eddie Boozan and me, for example. Eddie was an adopted boy in the family of an Irish neighbor. He was the product of an orphan asylum in Chicago, hot tempered and schooled in the rough and ready technique needed to keep his feet in the tumultuous life of an institution recruited from the tenements and streets of Chicago.

War broke out between us one day at noon recess for no reason that I now remember. A temporary armistice was declared, with the understanding that the matter was to be settled on the way home. As we trooped away from school at four o'clock, one of the enthusiastic ringside observers came near to betrayal by incautious reference to a coming event. A stern voice from the door brought us up short. There stood the teacher, J. C. Wright, a Civil War veteran and a gigantic martinet among us pygmies. (It was our theory that J. C. stood for Julius Caesar, who we knew was quite a fellow in his time.) To make a bad situation worse, he approved of my father and as a result was supposed to hold me in special favor. Smiling terribly, he looked us over. "Boys, I hope you don't mean there's been a fight."

All of us held the reasonable belief that a fight on the way home was outside the jurisdiction of the school, but no teacher agreed with us, and the power of decision was in the teacher's hands. The situation was critical, but stubby, freckle-faced Charlie Hicks, temporarily resident at the Porter Gregory farm, saved the day. Promptly and with a look of angelic innocence, he piped back, "No, sir." It was enough, but J. C. gave himself the luxury of a final warning. "You know," he said, "I punish fighting very severely." No one was disposed to argue the punitive theory involved in such a policy. Oh, we had the fight as scheduled, but the shadow of the schoolroom terror was over us. Our hearts were not in the battle and it was no more than a bloodless skirmish.

Few of our teachers had had special preparation for their work except that gained by previous teaching. But experienced teachers were likely to have ideas on salary, so a goodly number of ours were starting from close to scratch. The nearest normal school was a hundred and fifty miles away, and farm incomes gave little latitude for the higher learning. A few had had a year or two in the preparatory department of a small college nearer home, Monmouth or Knox, Lombard or Hedding, the latter two long since closed. County superintendents arranged "Teachers' Institutes," a week of meetings at the county seat, followed by an examination supposed to test the candidate's qualifications for a teaching certificate. The subjects were of course elementary and the examination proved little more than that the applicant knew more than his pupils.

In spite of these primitive requirements, we had some good teachers, a few at least. These were the devoted ones who really cared. I shall not forget one whose name is in my golden book.

Born of a family of teachers, growing up in an atmosphere of ideas and ideals, she brought to that crude, chaotic schoolhouse knowledge, understanding, and something that I was to identify later as intellectual excitement. Alma Carson was a great teacher in anybody's book. She died many years ago, but I am proud that before her life ended I tried to tell her of my gratitude to her for showing me that learning could be interesting. When she was in charge discipline was no problem. To lose her favor hurt more than one of Brother Wright's whippings.

To some of the parents, popularity with the scholars was prima facie proof of poor teaching, and a director in an adjoining district offered as a basic principle that no school should ever re-engage a teacher that "the kids liked." He was blood brother to the other man who held that no woman teacher could be worth thirty dollars a month. To men who worked from sun to sun and longer, teaching from nine to four, five days a week, was easy work. Our world in that day took no stock in the idea that a professional worker was entitled to higher pay because of special training and superior ability. What was so hard about teaching? Make the kids learn what's in their books and toe the mark in the schoolroom. That belief is still strong in some quarters where a college teacher's schedule of ten or twelve hours a week or less is regarded as ground for suspicion and legislative investigation. How can such a loafer employ his abundant leisure except in seditious activity? A favorite maxim of my youth was "Satan finds some mischief still for idle hands to do." Perhaps reading and thinking are forms of mischief.

Our schools had no social problems, at least in the modern sense. There were differences among us of course. Some of the families had more land or less money than others. Some were better farmers, but only a few had no land at all. Jerry Hawkins was one of these. Some time, not long before my memory began, the current of migration that had brought the Lincolns from Kentucky into Illinois years earlier brought Jerry and his wife to our neighborhood. By our narrow standards they were poor whites, slatternly, slovenly, thriftless. Else why were they landless? By whatever contrivance they had come to us, they had found a refuge in a combination log cabin and a rickety frame addition with a shed leanto, a survival from genuine pioneer days . Poor white he may have been, but Jerry was no idler. He was a good odd jobs man, a fair blacksmith, a useful hand at butchering time or threshing. He even went so far as to give an occasional hour to a ragged, straggling garden beside the Big Branch. Whatever else he grew, there were always a few tobacco plants to provide Jerry and his "old woman" with the long green for their smokin' and chewin.' Mrs. Hawkins's corncob pipe was condoned by most as a carry-over from the pioneer days when women smoked a pipe as a matter of course.

The Hawkins family were near neighbors of ours, only a quarter of a mile away through the woods, and the wife's friendly calls of an occasional pleasant afternoon, accompanied by her pipe, were a sore trial to my mother, proud of the neatness of her house-keeping. I might describe my era as extending from the pioneer pipe period to the modern cigarette, with feminine indulgence recognized at both ends and severely condemned in between.

One bleak winter, diphtheria, a dreaded scourge among us, attacked the Hawkins family and two of the children died. In the middle of a rainy, windy night Jerry came breathless to our door with the word that John, his only son, was in desperate need. Would some one go for a doctor? The nearest possibility was in Alexis, six miles away. Rain and wind and darkness were nothing when such a call came, but the water was over the grade on Henderson bottom, which must be crossed. Without hesitation Father waked Charlie, aged sixteen, and told him to saddle and start. Over the half mile of flooded road there was nothing to do but give the horse his head and trust to luck that there would be no drfitwood or barbed wire to bar the way. More than once his stirrups were in the water, but he made the hill beyond. It is to be noted that Doc Stanley in Alexis, roused from his warm bed, wasted no time asking about the state of the road or the Hawkins credit. It was in the line of duty, and he too saddled a horse and headed back with the messenger over the flooded road this time with growing daylight to help.

Roads are better now and the horse has become a museum piece in that township that once counted them by the thousand, but does the doctor of today answer the call regardless of weather or the state of the roads, or the blackness of the night?

Doc Stanley came too late, and a few neighbors gathered to dig the grave of little John. My brother long remembered that night, and that water stood in the grave when the small casket was lowered into it. No one received or expected pay for such services, beyond a few fumbling thanks. Next time the need might be their own.

There was a postscript to the tragedy of little John and his small sister. The township poor fund paid the costs of the doctor and the funeral, but somewhere Jerry found the money to pay for a black-bordered mourning card thanking the friends and neighbors for their loving kindness, presumably the work of some ambulance-chasing printer who studied the death notices in country weeklies. This foolish splurge earned the criticism of my thrifty mother who, incidentally, had provided the clothes in which the two small victims had been buried. Why did Jerry do it? Perhaps he found in this crude gesture some solace that he could not put into words of his own.

Racial minorities were unknown to us. We had no Negroes. Swedish immigrants were regarded as different and slightly amusing, but not necessarily inferior, although if the daughter of an "American" farmer married a Swede renter, the wives of the neighborhood united in sympathy with the bride's mother, apparently because Swedes spoke a queer language and had peculiar tastes in food. When these aliens began to prove that they could be as good farmers as the native born and their children began to take prizes in school, all was well.

As I look back I detect a curious phenomenon of religious prejudice. In our district there were four families of Irish Catholics living on "Cork Street," our name for the road on which they lived, bounding our farm on the north. Boys and girls were numerous in these families, and two of the Lee boys were my close chums and confidants. We walked together to and from school, we played together in school, we hunted rabbits, fished, or roamed the woods on holidays, when we could slip away from home tasks. We even compared our views of the present and our dreams for the future, some of them at least. And we never fought.

As to their religion, I knew that it was different from ours, but most of the time that was a matter of no importance. Only at confirmation time was a religious line drawn in the playground, especially by the girls. The sight of two or three Irish girls drawing apart from the rest and devoutly applying themselves during recess to the mastery of the catechism aroused our scorn. Viewing the separation as a challenge, we taunted them from a safe distance and hooted at their smug retorts. Once safely past confirmation, differences were promptly forgotten and the proper business of play went on as though nothing had happened. Brief religious exercises at the opening of the day were at the option of the teacher, the Lord's Prayer, a short passage of Scripture, no religious instruction. If there was protest in any part of the district we never knew of it.

My first experience with a Catholic service was the funeral of one of my schoolmates. Father decided that this was a good time for me to learn something of an important fact of life, the imminence of another life beyond this one, and I endured the slow drag over dusty roads from house to church as merely one more disagreeable duty. My memory of the service is dim, holding only my surprise tinged with shame when Father joined audibly and in English in the Pater Noster rapidly intoned in clerical Latin by the young priest. This was straining neighborly sympathy till it cracked. The loud wailing of the mother by the graveside shocked and embarrassed me, but I was reassured by the muttered disapproval of a couple of Irish neighbors standing near. Even to them keening was out of place in Illinois air.

It was an earlier death in the same family that gave me my first clear impression of death. The McGraths lived on a small farm of thirty or forty acres, father and mother and four children crowded into a tiny house even smaller than our own. Tuberculosis was common in our countryside then before doctors had learned the therapeutic values of fresh air and proper diet for the sufferers. At the first hint of the disease, the patient was put to bed in an airless room and hope was abandoned, a treatment calculated to kill the patient even if the doctor was wrong in the guess that often served for diagnosis. No care was taken to prevent transmission to others. In consequence none of the McGrath children lived to maturity. Tom went first and when word reached the school that he had died the night before a group of us, under the leadership of an older girl, went out of our way on the road home that night to observe the local ritual of a call of sympathy. Once inside the house we were taken in to see the dead boy, also according to custom. I was eight years old or thereabouts and the gruesome spectacle, especially the pennies on the eyes and the cloth tied around the chin to support the slack jaw, haunted me for days and made the nights when I lay awake in the darkness a time of horror. My fear of ridicule or reproof denied me the release that I might have found by confiding my obsession to a friendly elder.

It was politics rather than religion that created discord in the school, especially as election time approached. The Civil War was still being fought in District Number Four, where a number of the fathers had followed Grant or Sherman. It was commonly believed that the pedantic J. C. Wright, the schoolroom tyrant and bigot, still carried a rebel bullet in his body. Sometimes we wished that it had been more accurately placed. The Britts were in an anomalous position. Born a free Englishman, Father had hated slavery, as had most of his class in the old country, but he was a Democrat. How could I explain that? I couldn't. I could only bear my cross as belligerently or as meekly as the occasion seemed to demand. Father had not been a Copperhead, of that I was sure, but neither had he fought to save the Union. It was futile to explain that he was newly arrived in America when Sumter was fired on and that the war had little meaning to him. That only made matters worse.

The country school was an experience in practical democracy, but it made little direct contribution to our political education. We were born into a particular party as into a family or a clan, but no attempt was made to give even the older children any comprehension of political techniques or the issues involved. Candidates were names only and playground arguments brief exchanges of epithets. Democrats had tried to destroy the Union and the Republicans had saved it. At that time in the South children were undergoing the same indoctrination in reverse.

I had been vaguely aware of a contest in 1880 and of a feeling of hopeless disappointment when Garfield won. Be it said to my shame that my reaction to the assassination of the President the following summer was one of gratification. That would teach them to elect a Republican. When it dawned on me that the vice-president, another Republican, would succeed him, I resigned myself to despair. There was no beating the wily Republicans. To us, and to many of the voters, issues were meaningless. Free trade had a fine, brave sound, but civil service reform, the recovery of public lands illegally taken, the fading away of our navy were faint flickerings along the horizon. Prices of farm products were low and going lower, but few even of our elders could guess that in another ten years the low price of corn, wheat, cattle, and hogs, and the iniquities practiced upon us by the railroads would add up to a political issue of the first magnitude and focus our attention on what happened in Washington.

Chapter VII

"Reading, and Writing and 'Rithmetic"

THE SUBJECTS taught in our school were the traditional three R's, plus geography, a simple version of American history, and toward the end of my schooling, something called Civics. School boards of today would approve of that civics course as free from ideological taint or bias. In fact, it was free from ideas of any kind. All that I recall of it is that I committed the constitution of the United States and of the State of Illinois to memory. As the old phrase quaintly put it, "I knew them by heart." Whatever the origin of that term, I know that my heart had nothing to do with the task.

No attempt was made to explain or dramatize the Constitutional Convention in Philadelphia or to relate the document to our own lives. Teachers could not be expected to teach us what they had never been taught. For all the fuss and fury over present-day ignorance of the Constitution, that venerable institution is far better taught today than it was in my youth.

Learning by rote was the common practice in our schools. Knowing what the book said, instead of what it meant, was the test of excellence. I reeled off slabs of Barnes's *American History*, word for word, throwing in an occasional footnote for good measure. A phrase from a footnote on the Battle of Cold Harbor remains with me: "There was none of the pomp and glory of war, only its horrible butchery." I fear it was the rhetoric and not the implications that impressed me.

Sometimes the whole school read aloud or recited from memory in concert, after the manner of the "blab" schools described by

61

Edward Eggleston in *Hoosier Schoolmaster*. The intellectual value
of the practice is hard to perceive, but it did have the virtue of relief
from the boredom of spiritless routine. Five and a half hours of
physical inactivity and presumed study throw a heavy strain on
restless young muscles and nerves. The case for introducing the
playground elements of play and participation into the classroom
is a sound one.

"Spelling down" was a frequent part of the country school
day. Standing in a long line, we did our best—or worst—with
words given us by the teacher from lists in Webster's spelling
book, the famous blue-backed book that shared the spotlight in
American elementary education with McGuffey's readers for more
than two generations.[1] A miss sent the culprit slinking unhappily
to the foot of the line, and to finish the session at the head was an
achievement to be reported, modestly of course, at the family supper table. One of my mild triumphs was in my first encounter with
"phthisic." This odd combination of letters warned me to beware
and I consulted the teacher. Now I had seen the word and heard
it pronounced, and the field was mine. The general feeling of
the rest of the class was that to spell "tizik" in that absurd way was
a violation of the right of due process.

Spelling contests, "schools," were popular diversions for
adults in the winter months, often taking the form of contests
between neighborhoods. Such a match was arranged between
Tylerville and Coldbrook, a neighborhood centering on another
country church four miles away, and to my delight and trepidation
I was on the Tylerville team. I was thirteen and felt much as a
promising rookie must on being sent in to pitch in a World Series
game. It was "assessable" that won for me that time. Charlie

[1]The first edition of the famous Webster spelling book appeared in 1783
as the first part of "A Grammatical Institute of the English Language." This
was followed in 1806 by a small "Compendious Dictionary of the English
Language." Through his life Webster was a crusader against the tyranny
imposed by the overshadowing Samuel Johnson, especially the unnecessary
u in such words as *favor*, *savor*, *valor*. He fought also for much needed
reform of our copyright laws. Before his spellers vanished from the scene
a sale of more than 60,000,000 copies had been achieved.

deflated my pride by pointing out that the word had been mis-
spelled in every possible way before it came to me. Being the
youngest in a large family was an education in itself.

Did we learn to spell better than the present generation?
Probably. At least we had a better start in that direction, age for
age. How far my contemporaries held the advantage is another
question. Few of us learned anything of the reasons words are
spelled the way they are. Comparative philology was a term unknown to my generation and is not at home on the American campus even now. Reading was not a general habit in most families,
and correct spelling depends on constant participation in the traffic of words. Present prospects are not too bright. Our national
addiction to the daily paper, with concentration on comic strips and
the sports pages, gives little help, while radio and television are
effective aids to practical illiteracy. In time we may become a nation of people who have seen and heard everything, but can neither
read nor write. I think I'd better drop this argument. Before I
know it I'll be directing a sweeping verdict for the old-fashioned
spelling school. It had its points.

The name of the geography that we used, if it had a name,
has long since escaped me, although I remember clearly the name
and face of the girl who insisted that it was impossible to understand a map unless she sat facing the north. That girl would have
been sunk in a strange schoolroom on a cloudy day without a com-
pass. What did we learn from that nameless old geography?
Facts, my dear sir, facts: names of capitals, rivers, cities, mountains, lakes, chief products of, countries bounded by. Again my fly-
paper memory helped me out. I will to this day at reasonable odds,
undertake to name the capitals of the states and their locations, beginning with Maine, Augusta, on the Kennebec. If urged I think
I can render a plausible imitation of the singsong intonation of our
recital. If I miss, it will be somewhere after Colorado, that being
the newest state in those days. Our flag had only thirty-eight stars.
What good has this impressive knowledge done me? None that I
can discover. It hasn't even helped me to make friends and influence people.

Of geography as the study of the theater in which the drama of human history has been enacted we learned nothing; of the part that climatic change, glacial action, the amount of water on the surface or beneath it, forests, mountains, rivers, deserts, prevailing winds, rainfall, food supply, play in helping to determine human life and habits, not a hint. School geography could have been exciting. It wasn't.

Again, as with the Constitution and the history of the United States, no attempt was made to dramatize or humanize the countries of the world. People lived in those other countries, to be sure. Some of them were the homelands of our parents or grandparents. How did they dress? What kind of songs did they sing? What were their churches like? Their schools? What kind of games did they play? We knew little or nothing about such things except casual bits and pieces remembered by busy people who talked little of a past in another land. Neither textbooks nor teachers helped us out. An attempt to introduce costumes or songs and dances as part of the study of geography would have brought down the instant wrath of the whole district on the unlucky teacher's head. On this point at least the score for the little red schoolhouse was zero; entertainment was no part of the teacher's business.

I remember one small cartographic venture on my own. With some trepidation, fearing rebuke for wasting my time, I made an outline map of France that came out better than there was any reason to expect. To my surprise the result was praise rather than blame. The teacher even proposed to hang the map on the wall as a possible incentive to others. That was a bit too thick for me, but I saved face with my fellows by muttering something about adding a few touches before the map was exposed to public view. That did it. The matter was apparently forgotten, to my relief. At least the map remained unfinished. I had no wish to be the first to break orthodox practice.

The blackest page in my memory of the old school is the one that contains my record in penmanship. The man who made possible that chronicle of dismal failure was named Spencer, Platt Rogers Spencer. He died ten years before I was born, but his work lived after him. His slanted, graceful, colorless script was our model. No personal variations, no searching after individuality were permitted. Copy books were provided, the same for all ages, with a model in Spencerian at the top of the page, usually some appropriately moral sentiment. The exact distance letters might extend above or below the line was indicated by parallel lines, three spaces above for all capitals and *b*, *h*, and *l; d*, *p*, and *t* two spaces above; *p*, *q*, *y*, and *z* two below. The rest of them, the common people of the alphabet, did the best they could with a single space, although I seem to remember a measly quarter of a space latitude in height grudgingly granted to *r* and *s*. The reason for this concession I never knew. Perhaps Mr. Spencer didn't know either. That was just the way things were, a natural law possibility.

Try as I would, and did, pen gripped in the approved position, ink stains on fingers and face, blots distributed generously along the way, the best that I could achieve was a remote and unworthy imitation. Perhaps then, as later, I was in too much of a hurry to get something on the paper to pause for mere penmanship. What ever the merits of my case against Brother Spencer, I feel no debt of gratitude to him.

Old McGuffey readers are collectors' items now, but they were standard textbooks in country schools eighty years ago.[2] The college library that holds a complete set of the originals in good condition is lucky. Fortunately Mr. Ford, in his extensive delving into the evidences of our folkways, came up with the money for reprints of all six of them, and these at least need not be kept under lock and key. The only one that seems to have made any lasting impression on me was the Fifth, although the First is illuminative of the standard approach to the child mind in those pre-kindergarten days. Of course there is the alphabet, with no phonetic instructions. Children were left to deal with the paradoxes of use

[2]William Holmes McGuffey began the publication of his readers in 1836 and the series of six was completed in 1857. Meanwhile the compiler and editor held full-time posts as a college professor and administrator. At the time of his death in 1873, he was professor of moral philosophy at the University of Virginia. The sale of his readers reached the fabulous total of 122,000,000 copies.

and sound as they came to them, and the uneasy relation of *e* ano *i* remains obscure to most of us. One teacher did give us a limited formula, *i* after *l* and *e* after *c*, as in "lice." That was all very well for the forward *l* and *c*, but how about the other consonants? Being good Americans, we knew that *i* came after *p* in "pie," and Peiping was a long way in the future. "*Peignoir*" we knew nothing about. That's a foreign word anyway, and there's no accounting for foreigners.

A criticism of modern methods often heard is that children are no longer compelled to learn the alphabet and may grow old and die without ever knowing that *u* comes after *t*. Is that serious? Give me a minute to pull myself together and I can repeat the alphabet backwards, but the effective use of my mother tongue is still a difficult art.

The reading selections in that First Reader were harmless, but unexciting:

> Is it an axe?
> It is an axe.

Definite and reassuring, although even as five-year-olds we had discovered the axeness of the axe. Another gives a useful tip on social protocol:

> A fan for Ann.
> Can you fan me?
> I can fan you.
> You can fan me
> You do fan me.

That disposed of the fan. Finally a tentative appeal to childish sympathy is ventured:

> This old man is poor and ill and blind.
> He is led by his dog, a lit-tle red dog.
> Once he was a lit-tle boy, like you, but now he is
>   old and sick and poor.
> He has no son to take care of him,
> He must be led by his lit-tle dog.

The final paragraph of the book reveals that Mr. McGuffey, or his publisher, was aware of the desirability of preparing the child (or the parental) mind for the shock of buying a new reader next year. School boards furnished no textbooks or other student supplies in those heroic days. Our McGuffey admonished the youngster to "Take good care of your new book and give your old Reader to some child who is too poor to buy one." In the Britt family the recipient of this charity was the next brother or sister in line. I can testify that my Fifth Reader had come a long way down to me, perhaps all the way from the top of the family list.

It was this book that made me aware of something called literature, and I am grateful. The selections were about evenly divided between prose and verse, with two selections from Shakespeare. One of them was entitled "Shylock, or the Pound of Flesh," the conclusion of the trial scene in the *Merchant of Venice*, of course, although you'd never learn that from McGuffey. The other Shakespearean bit was the dungeon scene from the fourth act of *King John*, the dialogue between Hubert, the softhearted jailer, and the young prince. In neither case was a hint given that Mr. S. had written one or two other things. If we wanted to learn more than that about the greatest of English dramatists we must look elsewhere.

The theater was a thing unknown to us except by vague rumor, and was viewed by our elders as a luxury, distant, frivolous, and generally immoral. Once while serving on the jury in our county seat town, Father wasted an evening and two bits on a performance of *Uncle Tom's Cabin*, and viewed the expenditure of time and money ever after with unqualified regret. If there had been a hope that this parental disapproval would be transmitted through the family, it was marked for disappointment in my case. When I was somewhere in the neighborhood of twelve, Charlie and I broke bounds one unforgettable night and saw a play from the top gallery of the Galesburg Opera House—in which no opera was ever performed. It was the wildest melodrama, full of the standard hokum of battle, murder, and sudden death. For me it was a glimpse of another world revealed to me through the magic of the spoken voice, and the tinsel drama was something out of another life. By contrast the marvels of the silver screen, the radio, and television are commonplaces of technology.

Byron was another English name to make the McGuffey team twice, the "Night Before Waterloo" and "Apostrophe to the Ocean." Of the two I plumped for Waterloo and was given to intoning slabs of the rolling, stately lines in a sepulchral manner. I fancied myself particularly in the conclusion:

> Now Ardennes waves above them her green leaves
> Dewy with Nature's teardrops as they pass,
> Grieving if aught inanimate e'er grieves
> Over the unreturning brave, alas, etc.

Again McGuffey allowed merciful silence to brood over the identity of Byron. Omitting even the standard information that he had a club foot and quarreled with his mother. I seem to have made researches of my own on Byron. At least on a later day, when an unusually daring teacher, probably Alma Carson, was giving some of us a brief run-around in Greek legend and asked the name of the character who swam the Hellespont, I piped up promptly "Lord Byron." One of the girls who was about to mention Leander laughed in superior fashion. Fortunately the teacher knew of Byron's exploit and gave me at least honorable mention.

Hawthorne got into McGuffey only once, with "The Town Pump," from *Twice Told Tales*, and Daniel Webster was represented by an extract from his speech at the dedication of the Bunker Hill Monument, now an almost forgotten piece of Websteriana. When I refreshed my memory by a run through the Ford reprint of McGuffey, I was surprised to come upon the name of Rousseau in the Table of Contents. The selection bore the title "The Scriptures and the Saviour." In this case I found a brief note under the title: "The following is an extract from the writings of Rousseau, a French author of distinction, but a noted and avowed infidel." I am sure that reference to his other writings and his contributions to the Enlightenment would have been perfectly safe. None of us would have looked further, even if we had had a chance.

The choice from William Cullen Bryant was "Death of the Flowers," indicative of the poetic taste of the time. This was the generation that wept over *East Lynne and Thaddeus of Warsaw*. The purpose of literature was the cultivation of noble sentiments, and grief was evidence of refinement, especially if it were vicarious. It was bad form to weep over the hardships of every day, which were many, but tears over the sad fate of a character in a book provided a needed and safe emotional outlet.

It will be recalled that "Death of the Flowers" begins:

> The melancholy days have come,
> The saddest of the year,
> Of wailing winds and naked woods
> And meadows brown and sear . . .

It was the concluding stanza that brought the tears:

> And then I think of one, who in
> Her youthful beauty died,
> The fair meek blossom that grew up
> And faded by my side . . .

My keenest memory of country school most of the time is of boredom, relieved only by an occasional good teacher and always by the fifteen minutes of recess morning and afternoon and the blessed hour for lunch. The school day was from nine to four, and five and a half of those seven hours were segments of eternity.

Our lives were conditioned by weather, wet or dry, hot or cold, from a hundred above to twenty below, and we learned a few weather signs. I still assure myself that I can smell rain in the air long before the first drops fall, and I know that I could never forget the smell of the first drops spattering in the hot dust of a country road on summer afternoons. That was my legacy from my country upbringing, shared by few of the town breed. Years after my youth had been lost to me and I had been translated into a college authority, I remarked to a member of the faculty with whom I was walking to the college that it felt like rain. The harmless comment caught his instant attention and he asked for details. How did one feel rain or smell it? I couldn't tell him. I just did it.

Our weather lore was extensive and generally unreliable.

Some of it was embalmed in crude rhymes. "Rain before seven, clear before eleven." "Big drops, soon stops." "Mackerel sky, rain bye and bye." "Sunshine and rain, rain again tomorrow." Our research was highly unscientific and one lucky hit offset a lot of misses.

There were weather signs that were widely believed without ever being so rhythmically phrased. When you see cat or dog eating grass stand by for rain although the unusual diet meant nothing more than a digestive upset. The call of the blackbilled cuckoo also meant rain, and we called it a "rain crow" in consequence. When house flies clustered thick on the outside of screen doors in a hot summer afternoon, one did well to get under cover. Flies made it their business to know about rain.

Some of our worst winter storms were almost blizzards, never quite reaching the murderous ferocity of those in the western plains that more than once struck down and killed a man in the hundred yards from house to barn. No matter what the depth of snow or the force of the wind, it was the pride of the country school to keep open through the worst of it, and only definite illness could justify a plea to be permitted to stay home. Of course the weather was bad. What of it ?

Hailstorms were not uncommon but generally light, fortunately for farmers in that day when hail insurance was unknown. There was one, though, that really hurt. It hit in the middle of a night in May and came with a roar like that of a barrage of shrapnel. A cliche among us was that the stones were as "big as hens' eggs," but that time the cliche had solid backing. Chickens, young pigs, even a few young colts and calves caught in the open were killed, windows were broken of course, and growing crops beaten into the ground. The small cottage of George Terpenning, a neighbor, boasted a small leanto kitchen with a new tin roof. The morning after, George and his sons were on the roof soldering the holes left by the icy attack. We were sure that some of the stones had rivaled goose eggs.

We learned something along the paths between home and school. We could distinguish the three-leaved sheep sorrel that had a pleasantly sour taste from another plant very like it that was tasteless. We knew where to expect Indian tobacco, with its fuzzy, trilobed blossom in the spring, that we chewed for the tobacco-colored saliva that it produced, giving us a faint semblance of the maturity that we envied. A section of a dead wild grape vine was an almost lifelike cigarette if we could contrive to light the tip, and dried mullein leaves could be smoked in a homemade corncob pipe, with a stem cut from a wild vine that we knew as Indian Pipe Stem. Then there was Indian Turnip, a root that was very like the common turnip in appearance. The resemblance was less than skin-deep, as ignorant town boys learned to their sorrow when we persuaded them to bite into its bitter, burning interior.

Our woods were filled with wild flowers in the spring, for some of which we had names, bluebells, Johnny-jump-ups, little-boys' breeches, violets of course, honeysuckle, spring beauties. In early summer the delicate, fragile beauty of wild roses adorned the roadsides. There were many others for which we had no names. Wild morning glory was a pest in cornfields. We waged unending war against it, with only occasional tactical successes.

Although we were surrounded by woods our woods lore was scanty. We could make figure-four traps and once in a great many whiles might catch an inexperienced rabbit. I never did, but once I trapped our own barn cat, to his indignant disgust. We knew a rabbit track from that of a squirrel, and we were familiar with the straight trail of the fox. Coon tracks, too, we knew, delicate imitations of a baby's hand that appeared along shallow streams where there was a chance of crayfish, a favorite delicacy of Brother Coon. So far, we were self-taught Boy Scouts, no thanks to the school or our textbooks. Children of today are better taught, with deeper knowledge of the world around them than we were, gripes over "fads and frills" to the contrary notwithstanding.

The games we played were largely determined by the weather. Spring and fall were good for ball games, of course. Baseball was in its infancy and curve pitching was unknown to us, even as a remote mystery. Bats and balls were usually homemade, but small solid rubber balls were popular with boys who fancied themselves as long hitters. If there were enough players we "chose up" and played sides; this we called Town Ball. Otherwise it was One Old Cat or Rotation. Batters stayed in until they hit the ball, and base runners were put out by throwing the ball across the runner's path in front, or better still, hitting him with it. Some of the girls were as good players as any of us, except in throwing.

If it wasn't a ball game it was likely to be some kind of "Base," a variation of the game of tag. Pull-away was popular in our school, taking its name from the chant with which the game began, "Pum, pum, pull away. If you don't come we'll fetch you away." Play began with one player in the no-man's land between the two bases and all others lined up, ready to run across the danger zone to safety on the other base. The lone patrol in the center caught the slower, less agile runners and thumped them three times on the back in proof of capture. Then the captive joined with the patrol, and the game went on until all had been duly thumped—or the bell rang to call us in for the afternoon session.

Winter discouraged organized games, but a deep snow was hailed with delight. Then we built snow forts and fought fierce battles with the melting snow on milder days. Deep drifts gave opportunity for digging tunnels and making houses in the depths. Fox and geese was another snow game, a variant of tag. As a more manly interlude we followed rabbit tracks—seldom to the discomfort of the rabbit—or improvised toboggans from broken boards for coasting. The boy who could finish out the run still standing on his narrow footing was the hero of the moment.

There was little space for indoor games and in consequence rainy days had small popularity. It will be noted that no mention has been made of teacher supervision of our play. There was none. We heard occasionally of other schools where a young teacher joined in the games, but we never saw it at Science Hall in my time there. If possible the teacher went home for the noonday meal or to a nearby farmhouse that was home for the week, leaving us to discipline ourselves, and in general we did it fairly well. The play of children was not a matter for adult concern, whether at school or at home.

There was occasional interruption in the regular routine of study and recitation on Friday afternoons. Then from three to four we had "speaking." One after the other we dragged our feet to the neighborhood of the teacher's desk, and with nervous finger twitching at pants leg or skirt, we stumbled through a few stanzas of verse, pausing after each line to grope helplessly for the next. Modesty seems to have been overlooked in my makeup, and I found in these Friday afternoons opportunity for the display of what I fondly believed was but a prelude to a future as a platform figure of importance.

One such performance in which I rather fancied myself was culled from the Warren County *Democrat*, referring to something said to have happened in the Johnstown flood when an unknown rider on a big black horse rode down the valley warning the people to flee "to the hills for your lives."[3] I still think it was a pretty good example of topical verse in that time, and my rendition of it was well thought of, especially by myself. Only the opening verse lingers with me now:

> Hillsides were rosy at Conemaugh,
> Mottled and fragrant with Spring's sweet flowers;
> Her eyes laughed out through the golden noons
> And gazed through mists of the rainbow showers.

The last day of the school year was a doubly bright one. School was closing for the summer and there was a picnic in the school yard. Mothers and a few fathers came laden with fried chicken, jelly sandwiches, cake, pie, all the makings of an old-fashioned picnic—no hamburgers or weenies. Packed with food as we were, the program of declamations, songs, sometimes little one-act plays—we called them "dialogues" to avoid the taint of the theatre—held few terrors for us. On the way home, if we were daring and the teacher were unpopular enough, we sang a tuneless song of farewell, "Good bye, scholars, good bye, school, good-bye, teacher, darned old fool." We knew that summer on a farm was

[3]On May 31, 1889, an earthen dam upriver from the busy manufacturing and mining town of Johnstown, Pa., broke and 2,200 people died in the flood.

no holiday, but even work, some kinds, was better than an hour and a half of monotony on a hard bench in a June afternoon.

If I seem to speak with a touch of scorn, it is only partly sincere. There were many moments of enjoyment, but much too seldom, and they had little to do with the process of education. I recall a family saying when a child ventured to voice a dislike of some item on the menu, "You don't have to like it; you just have to eat it." That expressed a common attitude towards the business of schooling in our parts.

Chapter VIII

Old Fashioned Religion

RELIGION played a considerable part, a definite and controversial part, in the life of our neighborhood. Sectarian doctrines were closely held and the choice of a denomination was important. The issue at stake was vital, nothing less than eternal happiness or the unpleasant reverse. Hell and Heaven were literal states and the Devil warred constantly with God for the souls of men. There were several Catholic families in our neighborhood and a few Universalists, but Episcopalians and Unitarians were outside our world. Our prevailing beliefs were deeply rooted in the acceptance of the literal accuracy of the Bible and the lonely responsibility of the individual for his own salvation. The denominations competing actively for our support were in general agreement on these basic points, differing only on questions of procedure and technique. In our case there were two obvious possibilities, the Tylerville Methodist Episcopal church and the Coldbrook Christian church, usually called Campbellite by those who were not members.

Country churches, like country schools, were built by the people who were to use them. The rule of the time and place was. If you want anything done, do it yourself. Architects were unknown and unneeded. The plan was simple, four walls, a roof, and a floor, no vestibule or interior partitions, a rectangle thirty feet by sixty, or thereabouts, with a total capacity of around one hundred. The pews were wooden benches, with solid board backs at right angles to the seat, innocent of cushions or arms, and correspondingly uncomfortable. Families separated at the doors, women sitting at the right and men at the left, and when a small boy graduated from his mother's side to his father's, he had passed the first test on his painful way to manhood.

Heat was furnished by two large stoves burning soft coal, and in zero weather the temperature of the interior ranged from eighty above at close range to forty, or less on the fringes. Kerosene lamps dangling from the ceiling and set in wall brackets provided light when it was needed. The only break in the rule of rectangular rigidity was around the pulpit. The rail that set the preacher apart from the pews was of black walnut, gracefuly curved and polished by the hands that gripped it on the way to the pulpit. The black haircloth sofa on which the parson sat when the order of service permitted filled me with an uncomfortable sense of awe, and in consequence I still approach that kind of upholstery with respect and trepidation. There was no suggestion of an altar and no attempt at ecclesiastical symbol or adornment.

The total effect of the simplicity of the interior was one of harmony. This was a place of worship for people who lived simple lives devoid of decoration, and their church represented themselves. Decoration would have been an impertinence and a distraction.

When it came to a choice between Methodist and Christian, the decisive factor was often one of convenience.. Doctrinal divergences were on points that seem less than minor at this distance. For example, the Campbellites, officially, I believe, the Disciples of Christ, Christian for short, had leanings in the direction of the Baptists, but disagreed over the exact time at which the New Life began. Both denominations believed firmly in the necessity of baptism by immersion as a final guarantee of salvation and in the literal authenticity of the Scripture as the true Christian's guide. But when did the repentant sinner enter into his new life? The Baptists held that this took place at the time of conversion and acceptance, but the Campbellites made him wait for baptism.

The Methodists gave the candidate a choice between immersion and sprinkling, but memory reports that the Tylerville variety of sinner generally preferred the former as perhaps a trifle surer.

The neighborhood had no deep pools or lakes for the convenience of the faithful, and the ceremony usually took place in an artificial pond nearby, with muddy bottom and murky water, hardly an effective setting for the washing away of sins. On one occasion a slender young minister found himself under the necessity of dealing with a large and unwieldy woman who looked twice his size. Nothing daunted, the young man applied himself to the task. Three immersions were required and the first one went off successfully, but with the second the candidate slipped out of his grasp and disappeared in the muddy water to the accompaniment of much splashing and gasping. A sturdy farmer dashed to the rescue and the ceremony was completed to the satisfaction of all present, especially the unregenerate.

For most of us such minute controversies as the form and efficacy of baptism have long since been buried under a flood of more pressing matters, but in their time much fervid pulpit oratory and bitter recrimination were devoted to them.

The thirty years before the Civil War were years of intense sectarianism, especially in western and southern America, partly a revolt against the rigidity and dullness of some of the older faiths and partly stimulated by the wide belief in the imminence of the Second Coming and the Day of Judgment. Alexander Campbell, the founder of the Disciples of Christ, had rebelled against the strict government of the Presbyterians and sought a freer field for a simpler faith. Another sect of which we heard occasionally was the Winebrennarians, who included the washing of feet as part of the sacrament of the Lord's Supper. Baptists, Campbellites, and Methodists united in agreeing that this was carrying literalism to the point of absurdity.

Father's attitude was bewildering to me. Both he and Mother had been born in the Church of England, although I heard rumors of dissent somewhere in Father's family background, of which I knew little. As a new American he found himself in a predominantly Methodist neighborhood. Of the two possibilities, the Tylerville church was the nearer, and miles counted. So he became a Methodist. But Uncle Jim was even nearer to Tylerville and he allied himself early with the Campbellites, who were a mile and a half farther from him. It is interesting now to realize that it seems not to have occurred to either of them that active connection with any church could be avoided. Church membership was almost as much a part of citizenship as choice of a party and exercise of the right of suffrage. At least it was an attribute of status. Only the landless and the drifting could ignore it. There may have been agnostics or atheists among us, but I knew of none.

The Higher Criticism had not reached our ears, nor had the teachings of Darwin and Huxley, although there might be occasional vague references from the pulpit to the absurd doctrine that man was descended from a monkey. We did not know of Disraeli's diplomatic phrase in the meeting at Oxford, but we would have taken our stand with him "on the side of the angels."[1]

I remember a popular young Campbellite minister, viewed by some of his members as almost dangerously liberal, declaring with great positiveness that no scientist of any standing accepted the theory of evolution, and when I came home from college with a copy of The Origin of Species there was much concern in the family circle. Charlie disposed of the controversy by announcing in oracular fashion that the portrait of the author in the frontispiece looked more like a monkey than a man. Any monkey might well have been envious of the old scientist's flowing beard.

Our America was strongly Fundamentalist and Denominational. It was with a feeling of apprehension that I heard the same brother assert one day that he believed everything in the Bible except the story of Jonah and the whale. This, he declared, was more than he could swallow, as the whale had found Jonah. I didn't really fear a bolt of lightning from on high, but it seemed

[1]When the controversy in England over the evolutionary hypothesis was at its height, Disraeli, then Prime Minister, was on the platform in a meeting at Oxford seeking to reconcile the conflict between science and religion. Disraeli was a politician and not a scientist and his phrase was a masterpiece of diplomatic evasion that evoked gales of laughter from the audience: "The questions is this—Is man an ape or an angel? My Lord, I am on the side of the angels."

unlikely that such a daring statement would be allowed to pass un-
noticed.

There was much nervous curiosity over the exact nature
of the Unpardonable Sin. Did it lie in a word, an act, a thought?
Could it be committed ignorantly? No one denied the possibility of
an unpardonable sin and the dire effects that would surely follow,
but none of us knew what it was. Among us small fry who were
beginning to experiment in secret with profanity, it was commonly
believed that certain words were extrahazardous. (Our attempts
to understand the doctrine of the Trinity in terms of our own knowledge were futile, leading us into further confusion of thought and
argument.)

Church services were similar in all the denominations with
which I had any acquaintance. The order of service followed a
simple pattern of prayer, song, Scripture, exposition, exhortation,
collection and benediction. The hymnal that we used is remembered as a discordant collection ranging from Cardinal Newman's
stately "Lead Kindly Light" to numbers lacking both taste and
beauty. One of the latter is recalled with acute distatste. The
opening stanza ran thus:

> There is a fountain filled with blood
> Drawn from Emmanuel's veins
> And sinners plunged beneath that flood
> Lose all their guilty stains.

I fear there are churches in remote places where this is still a
favorite.

The terminal point of all sermons was the parlous state of the
unrepentant sinner. My acquaintance with the Tylerville church
began early before the dawn of conscious memory. Being Methodist, we were part of a circuit, survival of the days of circuit riding.
I seem to remember that our church was one of a group of three,
served by the same minister. The hard days when Peter Cartwright rode circuit over much of central Illinois, holding meetings
in taverns, schoolhouses, groves, even on the dance floor (so Cart-

wright reported were past.[2] Our preachers rode a circuit determined by the presiding elder of the district, and time and place
were fixed in advance. Usually they slept at home.

Even so, their lives were rugged enough. Our preacher's
home was at least six miles from our church, and miles over Illinois
roads were long. If they weren't buried in snow or mired with
mud, they were swathed in dust. The preacher's buggy, with its
torn top, its high wheels, and its plodding gait, could be identified
as far as it could be seen.

Our ministers came and went in frequent sequence at the
will of the presiding elder of the district. Three years was about
the average term, perhaps to prevent an incumbent from becoming
too much at ease in a particular Zion. In the case of Tylerville that
danger can hardly have been extreme.

From my point of view, the remoteness of the dominie was an
advantage as it reduced the liability of pastoral visits. These bearers
of the message took their jobs seriously. A call was an opportunity
to inquire into the spiritual temperature of the household. There
was usually a long reading from the Bible and a longer prayer.
When it could be managed without too much ostentation, the
preacher's appearance was a signal for me to merge into the landscape as quickly as possible. It took me a good many years to discover that a minister of the Gospel could be a friendly human
being.

The salaries paid ministers were as small as the members
could make them. At that, it was a good year when this subsistence wage was paid in full. In their practical moments, which
were most of the time, hard-working farmers rated preachers with
teachers as drones and parasites. Trained scholarship, acquired
by the expenditure of much time and money, was wasted. The occu-
pants of the pews wanted the pure milk of the Word, with no parade
of learning, and money spent in advanced study paid few dividends.
Less than a generation earlier, Cartwright and his kind had attack-

[2]Peter Cartwright was a pioneer "circuit-rider" who had most of central
Illinois for his parish. His autobiography is the classic authority for the
religious life of that time and place.

ed the idea of an educated ministry as a denial of the complete efficacy of the grace of God.

The heyday of the camp meeting was past by the time I came
on the scene, but a good many of the techniques that had distinguished that type of appeal were still in use. This was especially
true of the revival services "protracted meetings" held in the winter. For these occasions a special speaker, skilled in the prefervid
style of the earlier day, was called in and meetings were held nightly
for a week or more. The prime purpose was the saving of souls,
and the workers were not to be put off with the vague hope that
some good had been done. The proof of grace was the number of
sinners to ask for prayers or to come forward to the mourners' bench
at the climax of the evening. The inevitable peroration was the
"invitation." The sermon that preceded was merely a clearing of
the ground and a building up to this high point. The burning
anguish of the unrepentant sinner was painted in as harsh colors
as the speaker could command, with a mounting accompaniment
of Amens and Hallelujahs from the more devout in the congregation. Then came the invitation and the response, which had been
awaited with growing tension and curiosity. Who? And how
many? The answer to these questions determined the success or
failure of the meeting.

For the visiting evangelist such an evening was a physical
ordeal, as well as an emotional debauch. Perspiration rolled down
his face, and his short collar was as limp as a harvest hand's at the
end of a long day under the July sun.

How valid were the conversions accomplished in such an
atmosphere? It's difficult to say, but it would be a mistake to dismiss them as having little significance.

Revivals brought about a temporary cleansing and uplifting
of the religious tone of the congregation. Their faith had been
dramatized for them, crudely to be sure, but effectively, and for a
time religion had been made more real and important. The conduct of individuals was improved, at least on the surface, but it
is doubtful if the regeneration was more than skin-deep. Shrewd
horse traders would still bear watching and neighbors could still

quarrel over line fences. Our forgiveness of our enemies continued to vary with the depth of our enmity and our own enjoyment of it. Incidentally when contiguous neighbors failed to agree over the location or the upkeep of the divisional fence and resorted to the desperate step of twin fences a few feet apart, the narrow lane so formed was usually dubbed Devil's Lane, possibly an indication that even farm boundaries had a religious aspect.

While the Tylerville church building was erected after the Civil War, one feature of the Methodist practice which aroused my bewildered curiosity was the Class Meeting, apparently another survival of circuit riding and camp-meeting days. These were held on occasional Sundays when the regular preacher's other obligations kept him away from us. A prominent lay member, usually Bennet Snyder, presided. The program was a series of "testimonies" from the floor, interspersed with prayer and hymns. The form of the member testimonies was simple, usually an admission that the witness was a miserable sinner, much in need of the prayers of the congregation that he might walk more firmly in the faith. If the witness was a woman, and most of them were, the short, stammering appeal was apt to be accompanied by tears.

What was the purpose of the exercise? Was it a form of Methodist confessional, lacking the bill of particulars required in the Catholic faith? In pioneer days it had been a means for holding the congregations together and making them constantly aware of the need for self-examination. Did it still serve that purpose? Probably. Whatever the merits of the Class Meeting, the results were disappointing to a small boy, who found them vague and monotonous.

Sunday School was my particular sphere, usually held just before the regular service, presenting a problem in family logistics. If the family buggy, wagon, or sled provided transportation for all of us, it meant that I was hooked for a double session, which was something of an infliction for youth. As I grew older and acquired independent mobility, I was sometimes permitted to make the trip on horseback, with freedom to take off for home as soon as Sunday School was over.

The bright days were those in spring and early summer when we younger ones walked across the fields to the church and back again. Hedges and trees were green and the young corn was spreading its checkerboard pattern across the black earth. There were birds everywhere and awkward young rabbits scuttled away as we passed. On such a day I was prepared to believe that Sunday was in reality the Lord's day. There was a feeling of peace and quiet in the air, appropriate to the Sabbath, and a note of praise in the birdsong which I never heard inside the church, perhaps because birds do not sing through their noses.

There has been much discussion of the Sunday School as a form of religious education, with many wistful glances back to the time when all good children enjoyed Sunday School. That must have been before my time, or maybe I wasn't good. The printed program furnished by some central association somewhere—I should remember its name, but I don't—was about as exciting to me as the market reports in the county weekly. The teachers were local volunteers who stuck close to the subjects and questions suggested in the outline, with occasional excursions into amateur exposition of passages of Scripture. The limited knowledge that I acquired of the stately language of the King James version was all to the good. Of their value as great examples of literature, or of the part that this Bible had played in the history of humanity there was no hint. Such knowledge as I have of the contents of the Bible I owe more to my Sunday afternoon reading to my mother. At least I learned to identify those parts that were impressive to read and were suited to my limited powers as a reader.

In time our church acquired a small collection of books, carefully chosen by the central director of our religious destinies. I was hungry for books and I borrowed and read all that seemed to offer any chance of that vicarious experience that I unconsciously sought. It was no use. The blight of high moral purpose lay on all of them, and as soon as I was old enough I wrote Sunday School off as a total loss for me. I hope it's better now. Nowhere in my memory of the church or Sunday School of my youth is there more than an occasional fleeting glimpse of the devotion and mystery that lie close to the heart of religion.

Does that mean that I was callous or irreligious? Not in the least. I doubt if any normal boy in a normal environment is ever either one. The things that were said in church seemed to go by me, as though aimed at someone else. I'm sure that those leisurely walks across the fields, especially going home, gave me a clearer impression of something outside of and beyond myself, perhaps of the goodness of God, than I ever caught inside the church. I hope that the hours that I spent in church looking dreamily and longingly into the bright world outside are written down to my credit by one of the more perceptive angels.

Somehow I escaped the experience of conversion, again without conscious resistance or avoidance. I did not doubt it when I saw it made manifest in revival services. Something had happened to the penitents that didn't happen to me. I didn't long for it; I didn't dodge it; I just missed it. There may have been something of the rebel and the doubter in me even then. I recognized dogmatic authority when it was asserted from the pulpit or in school and bowed to it when it came my way, but I never submitted to it in my own mind. How did they know so much?

The sole concern of the church in our neighborhood was the salvation of the individual in another world. Life in this world was a testing and a preparation for a life hereafter. Man was a miserable sinner and the purpose of the church was to save him from the otherwise inevitable consequences of his sin. Nothing could excuse the individual for failure to see the light and to follow it. Foreign missions were a sacred duty because otherwise the heathen, even those without knowledge of the Truth or the chance to know it, were headed straight for perdition. That was a time of political corruption in high places and gross abuse of power in the business world, but our preachers gave us no hint of a social gospel. Sin was a personal matter, and there the responsibility of church and preacher rested.

Observance of the Sabbath was the generally accepted rule, but the practice has considerable variation. Of course, chores must be done morning and evening, or the machinery of farm life would break down. An obvious emergency, such as rain at harvest time followed by hot bright sun, might call for a full day's work in the field on Sunday to prevent over-ripe grain from crinkling down or hay from moulding on the ground. My own impression the first time such a rush involved me was of unusual virtue on my part. Psychologists may be able to explain this; my own conclusion is that somewhere in my subconscious was an unexpressed resentment on Sabbatarian controls plus a sense of daring in so ignoring them.

On normal Sundays, wandering in the woods and around the fields in pleasant weather was permitted, but if a swimming hole presented itself, it was advisable to make sure that your hair was dry before you went home. Only the more lax families permitted fishing or shooting. I seem to remember that games, indoors or out, were barred, but Sunday dinner after church was a good time for entertaining old friends. The Puritan practice of eating only food cooked the day before did not apply, and a Sunday dinner with guests was a banquet, with fried chicken and all the accompaniments. Anything less was an insult to company and a humiliating confession on the part of the housewife.

CHAPTER IX

What Did We Read?

W E HAD little to do with books. Even where the reading
appetite existed, as with me, there was no book money
left after the unavoidable taxes, interest and part payment of principal on the mortgage, the necessary items of clothing, farm
machinery, and occasional doctor's bills had been dealt with. Our
needs were few, but windfalls for luxuries were even fewer, and
books were luxuries.

A family Bible was necessary, of course, and somtimes, but
not always, a dictionary of some sort. A book of household remedies was fairly common, more often prescribing for domestic animals than for human beings. I recall a volume much in use in our
house, bearing the optimistic title *Enquire Within Upon Everything*. The spelling of the first word aroused my curiosity and I
was informed that it was like that in England where the book had
originated, just one of those international differences. The information that the book contained covered a wide range of topics, matters that could be disposed of briefly and concretely, the date of
the battle of Hastings, the inventor of the steam engine, phases
of the moon, the treatment for warts, and the distance from the
earth to the sun.

Book agents were occasional visitors and sometimes made a
sale. The books that came to us that way were apt to be collections
of prose and verse picked out of the uncopyrighted past and presented as "Gems" or "Garlands." We had a specimen of that breed
entitled *The Road to Success*, a neat little volume of five hundred
pages, "half morocco," calculated to spur and guide the young and

ambitious on their upward way. It came to us as payment for food
and lodging for man and horse for a night, and was a bargain any
way you looked at it. Following my general rule of tackling anything in print that came my way, I attacked this helpful number,
but without seeming to get more than the general idea that if I
didn't succeed it was my own fault. I seem to have heard that somewhere else.

There was another book in our small collection that pleased
me more, *The Voyage of the Fox in the Arctic Seas*, an account of
the experiences of the brig *Fox*, Captain McClintock, one of the
many expeditions in search of Sir John Franklin and his crew lost
in the Arctic seeking the Northwest Passage in 1845. The *Fox*
brought back evidence of the fate that had overtaken Franklin and
his men and I read and reread the narrative. I can still remember
some lines of verse that closed the chronicle of heroic failure:

> Then the gallant Crozier and brave FitzJames,
> And even the stout Sir John,
> Felt a sudden chill through their pulses thrill
> As the days and the weeks went on.

I was grateful to Captain McClintock for the relief he gave on
many dull rainy Sunday afternoons. How the book came to us I
never knew, but I'm sure it wasn't paid for in cash; perhaps another
night's lodging. There were other book agents, but most of them
came at the wrong time of day to leave any of their wares with us.

In due course I became a book vendor in a small way and for a
brief season. In my sixteenth year some wind of chance blew an
attractive offer my way. General William Tecumseh Sherman had
died the year before and an enterprising publisher had rushed to
print with a life of the general which stood in need of agents. It was
an irresistible opportunity in three styles, cloth, half morocco, full
morocco, "fully" illustrated, with liberal terms (25 percent) for
the agent. The season was convenient for the release of an assist-
ant hand on the farm, between sowing oats and corn planting, so
I took it on, armed with a sample cleverly made up to show the three
styles of binding at their best, with helpful hints on sales method
from overture to dotted line. My campaign opened with deceptive

success and I entertained dreams of affluence as I drove about the neighborhood, calling at farms where my family was well and favorably known. When I ran out of acquaintances and ventured among comparative strangers the discouraging truth came out; as a book salesman I was a flop. At least I learned that lesson young. But it wasn't a bad job while it lasted—light work, pleasant social contacts, and twelve dollars in my pocket.

A few books came our way as school prizes. One that Charlie picked off was Dana's *Two Years Before the Mast*. I read it through more times than I am willing to guess, and each reading was a new and exciting experience. Why a boy on an Illinois farm, a thousand miles from salt water, with no knowledge or tradition of the sea beyond the fact that his parents had crossed the Atlantic to reach America, should have found this book so enthralling is something of a mystery.

Another sea story of a quite different sort was *The Voyage of the Sunbeam*, written by a Sir Charles Brassey. The Brasseys were a "county family" in Sussex, near the parish of Netherfield that had contained the Bretts and the Fosters, but I'm sure that had nothing to do with our possession of the book, which recorded the pleasant cruise of Sir Charles and his lady around the world. I remember it only as a book and therefore better than nothing.

One of my birthdays was distinguished by a book as a present, Charles Dickens's *Child's History of England*. History of any kind, even in a school book, interested me, almost as exciting as fiction, but less orderly and probable, and this was my first look at our English past. If I had stopped with Dickens, my knowledge of England would have been superficial and inexact, but highly sanitary.

A more satisfying picture of English life was *Tom Brown's School Days*, borrowed from a neighbor. I can still remember how my mouth watered over the tales of toasting cheese and sausages at the great fireplace in the Hall and how my blood boiled over the indignities visited on the smaller boys by the tyrants of the sixth form.

Swiss Family Robinson came into view about the same time as

Tom Brown's School Days, probably another borrowing. This one also found great favor in my sight. But the brightest page in this chronicle of books that I discovered young is that which records my first encounter with Dickens the novelist. Dickens the historian had been wished on me, but his history of England had left me comparatively calm. His novels moved in and took complete possession. My sister Molly and I acquired a full set, including the unfinished *Mystery of Edwin Drood*, as a premium in some sort of contest, soap wrappers perhaps, or subscriptions to an otherwise forgotten publication. As a sample of the bookmaker's art it was close to absolute zero. The print was legible but otherwise atrocious, paper covers, page size about eight inches by twelve, two columns to the page. The paper was the cheapest possible for printing purposes, all in all not much of a collector's item, but the stories were all there.

The arrival of this prize was such an event in my life that the very day is written indelibly in my memory. It came in a big roll tightly wrapped in heavy brown paper, a bulky item in the homemade mail bag that I slung over one shoulder. The three and a half miles from postoffice to home dragged interminably, and my chores that must be done before supper were another eternity. But now I had an incentive. My usefulness on the farm, a controversial subject at best, took a bad slump while my first enthusiasm lasted, and that was quite a while.

I had my favorites among them of course, probably *David Copperfield* at the head of the list. My first entry in any contest over great lines in English fiction is that describing the finding of the body of Steerforth on the beach after the shipwreck: "He lay as though asleep, with his head on his arm, as I had often seen him lie at school." Mr. Micawber irritated me, but I forgave him all for his big scene with Uriah Heep, the prince of hypocrites. Next to David in my affectionate memory comes *Tale of Two Cities*. The scenes of Paris in the Reign of Terror were rather remote, and Sidney Carton's flimsy substitution of himself for Darnay, his French counterpart and rival, failed to convince me, but I was grateful for the pictures of inn parlors, with the bright fire on the hearth and the good food and drink waiting for the traveler. Mr. Dickens liked good food and the other creature comforts. Even I could see that.

Nicholas Nickleby held me all the way, although I found the helpful Cheeryble brothers so sweetly benign as to be scarcely credible.

Another favorite of mine was *Martin Chuzzlewit*. Sairey Gamp was a figure beyond price. Consider her final request as she settled down for the long night watch beside the bed of pain. "Just leave the bottle handy so I can put my lips to it when I am so disposed." Young Martin's sad experience as an architect in the frontier boom town of Eden taxed my credulity. Could America have been like that? Research in the history of town-building projects in the mushroom period of middle western history suggests interesting possibilities. Eden was Cairo, Illinois, pronounced Karo. The promoters of Cairo formed a corporation and sold stock, much of it in England in Dickens's time. Could the novelist have bought some of the shares from the mounting profits on his books? And were the chapters on Eden an equivalent for the dividends that never came? It could be.

One Dickens masterpiece missed me completely, *Pickwick Papers*. Only one scene made any impression on me, that of the famous breach-of-promise trial, and more particularly the advice the elder Weller shouted from the gallery to young Sam in the witness chair. Sam had been presented as "Weller." The judge is bothered by the witness's pronunciation of his own name as "Veller" and seeks light on the proper spelling. "Spell it with a Wee, Sammy!" shouts the father, to the annoyance and further confusion of the judge. The rest of the book bored me and I have never been able to finish it.

There were a few other books that passed briefly through my consciousness without leaving a definite trace, borrowings of the moment chiefly. One such was *East Lynne*, a novel that seems to have had a considerable vogue at the time. I tackled it as it came by, but without much success. I did wade through Jane Porter's *Scottish Chiefs*, another borrowing, and I found the pages that dealt with action highly exciting. The tears that Wallace, battler for the rights and freedoms of Scotland, indulged in between fights confused me, but I soon learned to skim lightly over such lachrymose interludes.

It will be seen that our knowledge of literature, as well as our exposure to it, was slight. Judged by academic standards our taste was low, but it would be a mistake to assume that we had none.

We read few newspapers and knew little of the outside world. Some of the great city dailies, the New York *Tribune*, Detroit *Free Press*, Chicago *Tribune*, published weekly editions that gave an occasional subscriber among us glimpses of a wider horizon. For years New York State farmers swore by, or at, "Greeley's *Tribune*." The old man had died, his heart broken by his defeat for the presidency in 1872, but he was still remembered. Our standard source of news was some small-town weekly, the Monmouth *Atlas*, Galesburg *Press and People*, Alexis *Argus*, or some other.

Modern newspaper standards provide no way of judging these journalistic pigmies. Most of their news was local and personal, furnished by neighborhood correspondents in Swan Creek, Cameron, Tylerville, or Dahinda. Through them we learned who had Sunday dinner with whom, or what married son in Kansas or Colorado was visiting the home folks. There were coy attempts at humor if the same horse and new sidebar buggy stood at the hitching post in front of the home of a popular young lady two or three Sunday evenings in succession. Obituary verse was another feature. The meter might limp and the syntax go astray, but the sentiments were irreproachable. Such superior critics as the New York *Sun* editors might find matter for derisive humor in these humble offerings, but our inglorious Miltons were unmuted.

The country weekly was tailored to country tastes. Front page news featured local happenings, and a fire in a local livery stable was more important than any but a major world event, such as the assassination of a king or the forming of a new alliance in Europe. Railroad wrecks were always good reading, especially when a local citizen was one of the passengers involved. Our standard journalistic fare was news about people doing the same kinds of things we did. "Sin is news," Mr. Dooley once remarked, but the country editor who had his eye on the ball dealt gently with local sin. The best issue of a local paper was the one that contained the most names of people known to the readers, and their sins were small potatoes anyway.

Editorial opinion was guarded except when partisan politics were to the fore. A presidential campaign was, of course, open season for the opposing party. To the Republicans all Democrats were, or had been, rebels, and to the Democrats, Republicans were plunderers of the public purse. Horace Greeley (who later ran for President on the Democratic ticket) once remarked that he wouldn't go so far as to say that all Democrats were horse thieves, but he had noted with interest that all horse thieves were Democrats. That was a sound political argument of the period.

The use of "boiler plate," or "patent insides," was common with the country press. Editing two or three pages with hammer and chisel saved time and type-setting for a hard-pressed editor. Syndicated columns serve a similar purpose for the modern dailies, often to no better purpose. At its average best the small-town weekly was a mirror of our lives and ways, and a file of almost any of them anywhere any time in the seventies or eighties should be a mine of material for the discerning student of our times and mores.

The first near-metropolitan newspaper that I knew was the weekly issue of the Detroit *Free Press* that came to us by the borrowing route. It was the feature articles that interested me. Front-page news may or may not have been important and well handled. I seldom read it. But the woes and tangled experiences of "Mr. and Mrs. Bowser" and the meetings of the Limekiln Club, both features signed by "M. Quad," were never overlooked. Later on I discovered that the personality behind the *nom de plume* was that of Charles B. Lewis. His humor was of the variety made famous by Bill Nye, Artemus Ward, and Josh Billings.

Much of the early newspaper writing of Eugene Field was of this order, a popular style of that day. Petroleum V. Nasby, with

whose writing Lincoln occasionally beguiled and bewildered his
Cabinet, was of the same school. It was a technique that relied
heavily on grotesque exaggeration of situation and phrase. The
practitioner nearer home was "Bob" Burdette, of the Burlington
(Iowa) *Hawkeye*, a good newspaper in a sleepy river town. Later
in life Burdette forsook the ways of sin as a newspaper humorist
and became an evangelist of considerable reputation. It used to be
said that newspaper work was an excellent training for anything
except more newspaper work, but few columnists have gone as
far as did Burdette.

I met another name in the *Free Press*, that of "Luke Sharp."
This writer took his work more seriously and in consequence I
have little recollection of details. In the late nineties his identity
became clear to me when I learned that Robert Barr, a successful
Scotch novelist of that time, had once adorned the staff of the *Free
Press* as Luke Sharp. From newspaper to novel is an obvious step,
and doubtless young reporters still dream of the day when their
novels or plays will free them from their daily drudgery, but few
achieve it as successfully as did Luke Sharp with his fourteen popular books.

Mention has been made of the borrowing of books and publications among us. There were four families on the neighborhood
mail route that my horse and I served twice a week, and reading
matter, to whomever addressed, came into the hands of ten or fifteen possible readers. No one of us read all of them, but I gave
it a good try. It was a curious melange that I sampled, religious
and farm weeklies, family story papers, *Harper's Magazine*, *Frank
Leslie's Popular Monthly*, New York *Ledger*, and the *Weekly
Witness*, a prohibition advocate.

My unvarying favorite was the *Youth's Companion*, long since
numbered among the magazines of the past. I was a faithful reader
of the *Companion* until I went away to prepare for college. There
is a special room in my house of grateful memories for the serials
by J. T. Trowbridge. The scene of most of his stories was Monroe
County, New York, the land of his youth, and through him I lived
the life of a country boy in a region where there were mountains,

lakes, catamounts, and an occasional wandering Mohawk. I knew
nothing of fairy tales, even of Andersen or Grimm, but with Trowbridge at hand I had no need of them.

Trowbridge even gave me a touch of schoolboy romance. One
of the older girls, her name was Elsie, found me a source of con-
tinuing entertainment. Her family looked with disfavor on fiction,
even of the *Youth's Companion* order, and many rainy days found
us in a quiet corner at lunchtime where I brought her down to date
on the latest installment of the current serial. Dazzled by recogni-
tion of my new social status, I ventured to tell her of my undying
affection. She smiled understandingly and patted my hand in
appreciation of the compliment I had paid her. And that was the
beginning and the end of that romance.

Once a year a catalogue of subscription premiums took the
place of the regular issue of the *Companion* and was almost equally
engrossing. There were appropriate rewards for any number of
new subscribers, from one to infinity, and a few times I was able to
pick off a small one. What a bewildering array of temptations that
catalogue revealed: books, magic lanterns, printing outfits, air
guns, snowshoes, toboggans—no cowboy boots or Hopalong Cas-
sidy sixshooters. It was my tragedy that my limited possible subscribers held me to the one or two-name selections; nevertheless,
I studied that catalogue closely. It comes to me that the subscription price for *Youth's Companion* was $1.75 a year, fifty-two issues.

That was the day of extremely free enterprise among advertisers, and it must be said that some of the religious weeklies were
favorite hunting grounds for dubious operators. Patent medicines,
promising relief from every imaginable ill, were abroad in the
land. Consumption, cancer, rheumatism, stomach disorders, were
cured quickly and at absurdly low cost. If you didn't know what
was wrong with you, somebody's Magic Elixir would cure you anyway. Fortunes could be made through the purchase of mining
stock, aiding in the release of a mysterious character unjustly held
in a Spanish jail, or a share in the settlement of a vast estate given
to Sir Francis Drake by his grateful queen after the defeat of the
Armada.

The Drake Estate fraud was a hardy perennial that persisted until quite recent years and may still be operating in underground fashion, for all I know to the contrary. I know that after I had left Tylerville for keeps, a buxom and plausible young lady appeared in the old neighborhood offering a minimum profit of a thousand percent to those who would come to the rescue of the British government by relieving them of the otherwise ownerless Drake Estate. With sorrow I record the fact that when she left she took with her some of the farmers' hard-earned money. She also took the ambitious husband of an old school friend of mine.

It was the good fortune of most of us that we lacked even the small amount of money needed to get in on the ground floor of the more attractive opportunities, but once my need for spending money led me into the clutches of a small-scale operator. It began with the receipt of an innocent looking family story paper. The fact that no one in the family had subscribed to it aroused no suspicion. Sucker lists were unknown to us. My greedy eyes spotted an innocent looking prize contest. The object was to make the largest number of words out of the letters contained in a single long word. I set to work with the family Webster at my elbow. Letter by letter I chased that word through the dictionary, checking and counting word by word. The grand prize was $10,000 and there were many lesser possibilities. I spent my winnings as I worked.

My list of words staggered the entire family, except Father who remained calm. In his experience a man got only what he worked for and not always that. He alone knew the amount of hard work that goes to the accumulation of $10,000 and had a deep distrust of short cuts. My list was surely in the money. I sent it in with high hope and my last dollar as "entry fee and evidence of good faith," was requested. The address was somewhere in Canada. In due course came a reply informing me with deep regret that I had missed top money, but that a silver tea set valued at $75.00 had been awarded me. I desired few things less than a silver tea set, and the request that I send $12.00 to cover the cost of shipping and packing reduced my temperature to something below zero. If I had had $12.00 would I have been wasting my time with the dictionary?

At this point Father swung into action. I had started something; I must see it through. Brief reference was made to teaching me a lesson, and Father advanced the money. We learned later that the Post Office was stopping all mail addressed to the Canadian philanthropist, but it came too late to save Father's $12.00. I have never been quite sure of the lesson I was to learn, but the experience weakened my faith in the printed word. Perhaps that was the lesson.

power. By my time the practice had become standardized and careful farmers kept a record of days owed by and to them. The basic unit of exchange was a day's work with man and team. Of course there were hired men, but not in the Britt family as long as the supply of sons held out. The going rate for a hired man on a year-round basis was twenty dollars a month and of course his keep. Sometimes the use of a horse on Sundays and holidays was added, or stable room and feed for his own nag, if he had one. In the active working season, April or May through corn-picking in late November, wages were higher. That was the time of year when the day began around five o'clock, or earlier, and ended when the chores were finished, perhaps seven or eight, adding up to an eighty-four hour week. At a top wage of twenty-five a month, the hourly rate worked out to seven cents, with "fringe benefits" of board and lodging for man and horse. Then as now, employers complained of high labor costs and slack workers and longed for the good old days to come again. The illusion of a golden age elsewhere in the past is a hardy perennial in human history.

The trading of work was usually confined to haying and harvest, with threshing included on a considerably larger scale. My haying debut covered three farms, perhaps three hundred acres under cultivation, divided among corn, oats, and hay in approximately equal proportions. Equipment was pooled and a careful account was kept of men, horses, and days. I was reckoned at half a man, an optimistic rating, but at least I was an essential worker. For the record it might be added that the entire working force of the three farms consisted of a minimum of ten horses and seven and a half men. A rough equivalent today with modern tractor machinery on the same area is two men and no horses. With horses eliminated the amount of land devoted to hay is much diminished. Soy beans now provide winter forage, and regenerate the soil to boot.

That first haying season held one large disappointment for me. My predecessor on the job that I now held had been the son of a small renter near-by who lived mostly by odd jobs. I knew that Billy had been paid the magnificent wage of fifty cents a day, and I

CHAPTER X

When Farming Was A Way Of Life

IT IS impossible for me to date my apprenticeship in farm work in terms of age. A farm family was an economic unit and each of us was a part of it. Only the very young, the very old, and an occasional chronic invalid were exempt. Even a three-year old could carry in chips for kindling, and the collection of eggs at the end of the hens' working day was clearly marked for the beginner old enough to understand that eggs are fragile freight.

This job would have been easy if the hens had been considerate enough to do all their laying in the henhouse that belonged to them, but they weren't. Most of them preferred the base of a haystack, a dark corner in the barn, or a clump of weeds secure from prying hawks. Gathering eggs was a daily contest between secretive poultry and the boy charged with the collecting. The daily round was not without its hazards. The urge to set would come upon a hen without regard to the number of eggs she had accumulated. Setting hens are notoriously bad tempered and the prying hand that tried to evict Biddy would be received with a volley of hard pecks.

Once at least I was caught in the toils of household law. The output of eggs had been sinking unaccountably and I was put on notice that the trend must be reversed. The dilemma was unescapable. More eggs or else! Before I could arrange my defense or construct an alibi an outlaw or two emerged from their hideouts brazenly convoying broods of fluffy chicks. They had achieved the ultimate hennish triumph, a hidden nest and a growing family, but I was sunk. The memory of that thrashing rankled for a long time. Who was I to match wits with a hen intent on following Nature's law? My offense was the greater because I received a bonus of one cent a dozen on the total take and I had failed to follow my own obvious self-interest. Adam Smith didn't know about hens evidently.

A few times we added turkeys to our poultry operations, and finding turkey eggs was beyond the ability of a better man than I was. Turkeys were close to the wild and the hens wandered widely in search of a satisfactory spot for a nest. Fortunately the eggs were not rated high in our kitchen and had value only as they developed into more turkeys. Ours were never much of a success. Hawks, crows, weasels, and rats took heavy toll of eggs and young, and in spite of their recent wild origin, cold wet weather could decimate the flock. Roast turkey was not a traditional Thanksgiving or Christmas necessity for us, unless we had grown our own. We may have brought one home from the butcher's for a special occasion, but I do not recall anything of the sort. Here and there farms might try ducks or geese, sometimes with a staid old Plymouth Rock to do the setting and rearing, but in such a case the amphibious habits of the children brought the foster mother to the verge of nervous prostration.

Somewhere toward the end of my first decade, I became the distributor of mail for the three families that lived in fairly close order along our back road. Except in muddy or cold weather, this was almost pure joy, a pleasant ride along lonely roads for the seven-mile round trip. That was a good time for dreaming, for the staging of wild adventures in which the dreamer, of course, always played the leading role. I was by turns a dashing cavalryman, a wandering cowboy, a highwayman, riding with Jesse James perhaps. By this time Jesse was in a fair way to become a folk hero and we knew snatches of some of the ballads built around his exploits:

> Jesse James was a thief, though kind to the poor,
> And for money he never suffered pain . . .

and of course the cryptic last lines:

> 'Twas a thief and a coward
> Who shot Mr. Howard
> And laid poor Jesse in his grave.

James was calling himself Howard at the time of his death. H was shot in the back by a member of his own gang, one Bob Ford.

Custer was an intriguing model after 1876, but his death i the Little Big Horn fight presented difficulties. It was not eas for a small boy to find satisfaction in posthumous fame. He wante to hear the cheers and the songs and to wave modestly to the crowds Death, even the death of a hero, interfered with that pleasing prospect.[1]

My progress from the humble status of a doer of light chores to the level of a full hand with a team, which was the ultimate in manhood, seemed unbelievably slow, but in reality was surprisingly fast, measured in years. Of course the size of the boy had something to do with it. The bigger the boy, the sooner in the field with a team for a full day's work, but if he hadn't made a beginning by the time he was twelve the adult world took a gloomy view of his future. I was of a size known as "small for his age"—still am in fact. My first intimation of this discouraging fact came from a heartless clerk in a clothing store where I was being looked over for a new suit. With that bad news the acquiring of a new suit lost its glamor, even with a necktie or a pair of suspenders to boot, as was the local custom.

I associate my first knock on the door of full status in the field with the haying season in my eleventh year, although it may have been a year earlier. I was assigned the job of driving the horses that operated the stacker in the field and the fork that hoisted the hay from the loaded wagon to the haymow in the barn. Whatever the year, it was also my introduction to the neighborhood practice of "trading work."

In reality, trading work was a survival of the pioneer custom of mutual aid for major jobs, requiring extra men and horse

[1]Custer and all the officers and men of five troops of the Seventh Cavalry were killed in a fight with the Sioux and North Cheyennes on June 25 1876. There were many investigations and much bitterness over this affair The Little Big Horn fight was the best of all the Sioux battles—and the last

held that comforting thought while the haying lasted. To be sure I belonged to one of the participating families and my labor was logically a part of the common contribution. Nothing had been said to the contrary. But maybe this particular job was in a special cash category. It had been so in the case of the late Billy. Besides I was the only fraction in the score and fractions, even tractable halves, complicated the records. It was a vain hope. The haying ended, the equipment was put away and all hands turned to other tasks, but I had counted the days and multiplied them by fifty so often that I felt myself the victim of a barefaced fraud. I did not know then that Billy's wage was paid to his father to do its bit toward the balancing of a slender family budget. We were both the helpless victims of a remorseless economic machine that had only one object, to keep going. If there is a better object I have not found it.

By the time I had graduated from the status of a water-boy self-binders had ousted the old reapers from the grain fields, so I escaped the binding by hand, although I had learned to throw the band around the bundle and tie the knot.

Threshing time was a special occasion with us. A threshing machine was too expensive for a single farm and called for some experience in the operation; hence threshing was a contract job. A mechanical-minded farmer would contrive the purchase of a rig that served a large number of farms, sometimes working far into the fall. The early machines were run by horsepower. Steam, another step in the mechanization of the farm, came much later.

The machine crew was usually three men, with the "feeder" as the key man of the outfit. As he did his work well or ill so went the day. He stood at the feedboard slanting down to the toothed cylinder which did the threshing. The rest of the mechnical process was the separation and sifting of the grain from the straw and the chaff. A feeder's carelessness or incompetence could stall the machine when it was running full, a cardinal offense involving a slow process of clearing it by hand. At each side of the feeder were tables to which bundles were pitched from load or stack. There also stood the bandcutters, armed with sharp knives. The cutter's duty was to cut the twine band with one quick slash and shove the loose bundle toward the feeder. A second try was a confession of incompetence and might gash the hand of the feeder as he reached for the grain. It might also earn the cutter a backhand blow that would put him on his back on the ground.

Threshing by machine had its peculiar dangers. When oxen trod the ripe grain on the threshing floor, or men and women beat it out with flails, the risk was about the same as walking along a country road before the demon that hides in gasoline was unleashed. With the threshing machine came the danger of mutilation of the feeder's hands by the spinning cylinder with its curved teeth. I never saw it happen, but the danger was there and every threshing season brought its minor injuries charged to the machine. The substitution of steam for horsepower brought another peril. Many of the engineers were self taught, and engines were kept in use as long as they held together. Aging boilers sometimes let go when an indifferent engineer failed to watch his steam gauge. That happened in a nearby township and two men were killed in the blast. The life of the farmer was simple and generally peaceful, but not always safe.

Bandcutting was traditionally a boy's job, and I can testify from experience that it was a tough one. When the machine was running well there was no time for a shift of position, or even a glance away from the stream of bundles that cascaded from the load. Butts raked across his face, sweat trickled into his eyes, his legs ached from the unvarying strain, his skin itched from the chaff that sifted down inside his shirt—still there was no relief. He must keep his attention fixed on the one test of his work, cutting the bands. He was the slave of the hungry machine. The rule of his life was one band, one slash. By the end of the day he was covered with dust and chaff from head to foot and his legs were wooden. Boy's work maybe, but the thought that he was part of a threshing crew, almost a man working alongside other men, was compensation. Hot as the nights were in summer no sedative was needed when he slid between the sheets.

A full crew might demand fourteen men in addition to the

machine tenders, four with teams to haul bundles, two with other teams to haul the grain to granary or elevator, two to pitch the bundles to the loaders, two bandcutters, three to stack the straw at the tail of the thresher—another hot and dirty job as a good setting demanded that the tail be downwind to prevent the chaff from blowing back on the other workers—and one man to hoist the half-bushel measures into which the grain ran and dump them over the endgate of the waiting wagon. As a full measure was pulled away from the spout down which the grain came, it clicked a trigger operating a tallying device. The owner of the rig was paid by the bushel and the tallybox was the complete evidence.

The aristocrats of threshing were the men who hauled the bundles from field to machine.   It was their happy lot to work in clear air and sunshine, except for the brief period of unloading. In the occasional intervals to repair a minor breakdown talk went round the group. The stories that were told were not always of the bedtime variety and the jokes that were played were crude and rough.   These were rough men and they talked as rough men do.

Dinner was the crowning touch of the day. Housewives spread themselves for threshers with fried chicken, boiled beef or pork or both, mounds of mashed potatoes with gravy, fresh vegetables, at least three kinds of pie and as many of cake. The team ate as hungry men eat everywhere, greedily and with complete absorption in the business in hand. There was no table talk. Words were used sparingly in the frequent requests for seconds, "Beef!" "Potatoes!" sometimes with a "please," but no more. Table manners were at a minimum. A knife was a convenient shovel, as I learned to my embarrassment when attention was called to my effeminate habit of eating pie with a fork. The sole concern of the moment was with food, as much and as quickly as possible.

Dinner for threshers was the acid test of a good housewife. Unless the food was good and abundant, the verdict was against the cook and there was no appeal.   There was one farmer with a special reputation for penny-pinching.   Fortunately his threshing job was usually a short one and with careful planning the schedule could be juggled for the omission of the dinner hour at this farm. It was said of this farmer that he sold what he could, what he couldn't sell he gave to his family, and what the family wouldn't eat he fed to his hogs. It was whispered that what his hogs declined he saved for threshers. Our judgments may have lacked subtlety but they were definite. It should be added that I remember no other such case.

If explanation is needed for these details, there is justification for them. We were seeing the early steps in the mechanization of the farm, one of our more profound revolutions. The internal combustion engine and gasoline speeded up the rate of change, but they did not start it. Cyrus McCormick was not the first pioneer in farm machinery, but his machine and its descendants made possible the mass production of wheat on the level, treeless western plains. Consider a few facts: before McCormick it was estimated that three man-hours were required to sow, reap, and thresh a bushel of wheat. What is it now? Less than that many minutes. There is the complete answer to the wistful question, "Why are the boys leaving the farm?" The machine has driven them off; the farm no longer needs them.

Gasoline plus machines displaced men and horses and stepped-up production. The cost of the machine increased the capital burden on the land and edged the little man with the narrow margin nearer the point at which he would cease to be a farmer. With the growing production of staples, made possible by more efficient machinery, the farmer must look farther for his market. Did the market come first or the machine? How about the chicken or the egg? Again a fact or two: when eighty per cent of us lived on the land, there were only twenty per cent of helpless town dwellers to be fed. Now the ratio is reversed. The great staples, wheat and cotton especially, seek a world-wide market. Today far fewer farmers proportionately feed far more of the helpless, who must be reached through a complicated chain of transportation, brokerage, insurance, import duties, and foreign competition. Those who think that the "Farmers Revolt," culminating in 1896, was an absurd uprising of revolutionary radicalism, spurred on by glib-tongued demagogues, should read the history of American farming from 1865 to date.

The farmer's work was hard and his hours were long. Probably that is still true, although there are differences and degrees of hardness. We stumbled along behind plow or harrow, our feet sinking in the soft earth, blinded by dust blown by the never failing wind in dry weather or drenched and chilled through and through by the showers that rode in on the wind. The pace was slow and the days seemed endless, but monotonous as the work was, endless repetition of the rounds of the field, it was not always disagreeable.

Plowing was one kind of farm work that I liked, in spite of its monotony. Physically I was on the stubby side and when I plowed my first furrow, *aetat* 12, I found myself reaching up to grasp the plow handles which were almost at the level of my shoulders. Dragging the plow around at the end of the furrow was a performance that amused everyone except the young plowman. Our plows cut narrow furrows, fourteen, sixteen, or eighteen inches wide, as the case might be. The eighteen-inchers were the giants calling for three horses working abreast. Driving a three-horse team was one of the jobs that separated the men from the boys. The fourteen-inch with two horses was my lot, until increased strength and stature promoted me. Horses, too, soon learned that dragging a heavy plow around and around the field was no pastime and the hot blood of youth cooled rapidly. Runaways in plowing time were few.

In the slow plodding behind the plow from seven in the morning to six at night with a short hour out for midday dinner—nothing so scanty as a "lunch"—there was a kind of "blissful anodyne" that few poets have known anything about. Birds were quick to sense the possibility of worms along the furrow, and blackbirds, robins, and field sparrows answered the invitation. The air was filled with the unforgettable fragrance of freshly turned earth. The sun shone and if a soft wind brought assurance of spring the days were not always too long.

Of course there were rainy days. The sun did not shine

always, even in the days of my youth. But days when showers and sun alternated might present problems in practical ethics. How long or how hard must it rain to justify quitting for the day? How wet is too wet? Clearly to be caught by bright sunshine on the way to shelter would be a tactical error and a species of too-easy sur- render. How to be sure? Authority said stick it until you're forced to quit. More than once the boy laborer found himself dragging through a long day, never wet enough to quit or dry enough to be comfortable. That state passed for humor in those simple days. Truly it is the minor choices of life that make most of the trouble. What to do now, this very minute, that's the hard question to answer. The big decisions are usually made for us by unescapable circumstance; at least that's the way it seemed to the boy on the farm.

Plows and harrows were growing larger and gang plows were appearing on the larger level fields, sometimes cutting three fur- rows simultaneously with three or perhaps four horses hitched abreast. We began to hear of disks doing the work of plow and harrow combined, but horsepower still set the pace and the scope of the machine, and men still walked in the furrow and behind the har- row. Thus it had always been and thus it would be as long as men farmed the land—and that of course is always.

Motorists careening along concrete highways through the corn country in early June exclaim over the checkerboard pattern of the rows of young corn in the fields and wonder idly how and why. The how of it is simple, the corn is planted that way. The early corn planters required that someone of light weight, often the boy of the family, sit on the front end of the machine and operate a lever releasing a few grains of corn at the exact instant of passing a cross mark previously made by dragging a sledlike framework across the field. Pulling the lever too soon or too late produced zigzag cross rows and an erratic checkerboard design. The whyness of the pattern was even simpler, merely that the cultivator plows that followed when the corn was up might work both ways in the un- ending war against weeds.

It was a simple device that ousted the boy from his uneasy seat

on the front end of the old planter and substituted precision operation for the haphazard guessing of the old hand method. A product of the old neighborhood, almost a neighbor of ours, made
the first "checkrow." In young manhood George W. Brown had
been a carpenter and a good one. A house of his buildings stood
long on a farm not far from ours. I saw it pass in its life cycle from
a home for a family to its last stage as housing for tools and farm
miscellany. To the day of its demolition its frame was sound and
strong, and the amateur wreckers made bitter complaint of its stubborn mortised joints and wooden pins.

Before that old house went on its way there was a brief interlude when it housed a secret organization known cabalistically as
the BYMH. Only the members knew for sure that these letters
stood for Brave Young Men of Hardscrabble, that being the term
applied in wry humor to our neighborhood. The purpose of this
society was vague, if in fact there was any. There were rumors
about that the old house was haunted. A farmer returning late
from town swore that a ghastly specter appeared at the roadside
and sent his team dashing down the road in panic, but the man's
habits were not always of the steadiest and his evidence was not
taken seriously.

One nocturnal adventure a charter member recalls. That
was the night we cooked the old hen. A battered cookstove and
an iron kettle were at hand; chickens could be found anywhere.
So the necessary missions were sent out, one to find some salt, another to pick up wood for the fire, and a third to catch the necessary fowl. All these things were easily done—we found the objects
of our search at our own homes, but there was a catch. How long
should the bird cook? There was no cook among us. The hen was
old and tough and we were in a hurry. In duty bound we made
a pretense of eating but the feast was an anti-climax.

Young Brown, growing up in that land of cornfields, saw
where the machine could take the place of a man, to the inventor's
profit. The industrial revolution was at work among us, and Brown
became the chief magnate in the small city of Galesburg, its first
millionaire. It was my privilege once as a small boy to shake his

hand, and I was vastly impressed by the ornate watch chain draped across his ample front. I had been identified as the son of Ed Britt, and the great man made curt acknowledgment: "I don't know Ed Britt and I don't know his son." It was my first contact with economic royalty and I was not pleased. A great grandson acquired a small local reputation for his skill in producing a musical effect by snapping his fingers. When the old man had snapped his fingers men jumped; when great grandson did it, they danced. One of Time's little revenges!

As machines multiplied on our farms, factories to build them sprouted in our county towns. Brown's was only one of several. Monmouth, our county seat, could boast two plants turning out corn cultivators, and Galesburg was the home of the Avery implements, later shifted to Peoria.

While we were being modernized and mechanized in ways we scarcely understood, a part of our minds still clung to the old. We remembered that the Indian had planted his corn when the white oak leaves were the size of a squirrel's ear. That was not our only calendar, but it helped. With us May twentieth was the latest safe date for planting our corn. Corn planted later was a tempting of fate in the shape of an early September frost.

June was the month for plowing corn. Day after day, horses and men plodded to and fro across the fields with the cultivators. Early settlers had fought with a single plow and horse, working one side of a row. Some forgotten genius, weary of the endless plodding that this involved, hitched two single plows to an axle connecting a pair of wheels. Now he could deal with both sides of a row at the same time, and the measure of a day's plowing was thereby doubled. Cultivating called for constant vigilance. There was no furrow to guide the team, and when the corn was young the shovels must get rid of the weeds and at the same time avoid burying the corn. A strong hand was needed on each plow handle, and when guiding of the horses was called for it must be accomplished by a quick twitch of the lines looped around the plowman's waist.

The second plowing was always crosswise, following the

rows that the faithful checkrow had provided. There were never
days enough to quite keep pace with the weeds, of which there
were many kinds, some worse than others, but all bad. The most
pestiferous of all was the wild morning glory, its roots seeming to
stretch as far underground as its vines above, choking the growth
of the young plants. As soon as the first plowing was over the
next began, and so it went until the corn threatened to reach the
level of the horses' backs The last time over was "laying-by," and
the shovels were set to throw a ridge of earth along the row as a
last gesture of defiance to the weeds. If you couldn't do that by
the Fourth of July you were a lazy farmer, or an unlucky one.

Late June days in the corn belt are often hot, and there were
moonlight nights that saw the cultivators on their rounds to escape
the killing heat of the afternoons when horses and men walked
almost shoulder deep in growing corn. Those were the "growing
days" that farmers prayed for, and we repeated the fixed belief
that on still nights keen ears could "hear the corn grow." It was
fancy of course, but I remember such windless nights when I seemed to catch a faint rustle in the fields where the leaves of corn hung
moveless. It was of such nights that an old friend, Rollin Kirby the
cartoonist, long a voluntary exile from the corn belt as was I, was
thinking when he voiced his feelings in colloquial fashion about
the land of our youth: "Country that's fittin' for corn ain't fittin'
for human beings."

The last chapter of the yearly epic of the cornfields was the
hardest, corn "shuckin'." The Yankee farmer cut his corn green
and let it ripen in the shock, saving the husking for a later day.
Husking bees, with occasional red ears and a pretty girl or two at
hand to pay the forfeit, probably did take place in New England.
We had our share of red ears and pretty girls, but no husking
bees. We did the husking—"shucking" we called it—in the standing corn with a husking pin strapped to the fingers of the right
hand, with a sharp point projecting to tear away the husks from the
tip of the drooping ear. Top hands could do the trick in three swift
movements in such close succession that they seemed almost simul-
taneous, ending with a quick toss that landed the ear in the wagon.

With such a picker the ears beat a quick tattoo against the high backboard of the wagon box. If there was a boy about, the team walked astride the first row, the "down" row, and picking this became the special province of the boy. A picker had need to work at top speed if he was to bring in a hundred bushels by the day's end, which was the final proof of expertness.

It was hard work, with no aspects of romance or high adventure that I was able to discover. Corn-picking didn't dramatize easily. It began in November on cold frosty mornings, or worse still, in misty rain with a hint of snow to come. Days in the field began before sunrise and ended when the light was growing dim. Horses were fed, curried, and harnessed, cows milked before the picking began, and evening chores were done by lantern light. After a day or two, hands began to chap and bleed, as only the most sensitive wore gloves. The standard treatment for hands in need of care was melted tallow—tallow and fortitude.

In early days the dead cornstalks had been cleared away while the ground was still frozen by dragging a long pole, or better still a length of railroad iron, across the field, breaking down the stalks for the plowing. Then horsedrawn stalkcutters came in, bringing with them a special danger for the driver perched above the knives. Sam Armstrong, a near neighbor, was drawn into the deadly knives and mortally injured. It was long before the rest of us forgot that tragedy.

I had an adventure of my own with a stalkcutter. I was driving my weary round in the late afternoon of a long day when something startled my sleepy old team and a sudden lunge broke the tongue of the cutter, and I found myself perched on a lurching platform trying to control a team that had gone mad. It was time to abandon ship and I dove over the wheel. For an agonizing moment I found my feet tangled in the lines with which I could no longer control my runaways. Then I was clear and stood to watch team and cutter disappear over a hill where the cutter was dumped contemptuously into a small ditch. It was safe but not by much, and I cut no more stalks with that murderous machine.

Chapter XI

How The Land Fed Us

T HE CALENDAR of the farmer's year held more than the major items of plowing, sowing, reaping, and gathering. Important as these were, the framework of farming as a self-supporting institution, there were other corollary and subsidiary activities and functions that could not be ignored if the occupation was to become also a way of life. It was necessary that the farmer should eat and that, so far as possible, the farm should provide the food. The staples of corn and oats were for the market, the means by which money, real money, came to us, sometimes directly, more often in the form of fat hogs and cattle. We grew our own pork, most of our beef, and all of our poultry. Meat was the backbone of our diet, but fruit and vegetables were important accessories.

On many farms the garden was the obligation of the women after the ground had been plowed, but not with us. As soon as there were grown sons to take care of the main crops, Father turned to fruit and vegetables, and every year a convenient plot was set aside for his special use and benefit. A one-horse shovel plow and a docile old mare made up his mechanical equipment. The rest of it was spading fork, rake, and hoe. The old mare was slow and Father's temper was quick, so everyone within a quarter of a mile knew when the garden was being plowed.

Potatoes were basic on the table and hence in the garden. There was one season of the year when my contact with potatoes was intimate and grievous. That was in the early spring when the cellar bins in which they were stored began to show signs of sprouting. Then it was made clear that there was a job waiting, to rub

113

the sprouts off before the tubers began to soften and decay. Cellars are dark and gloomy places at best, and our potato bin was always in the darkest and gloomiest corner. Fate usually decreed that the day of my solitary confinement with the potatoes was also the day selected by my brothers for fishing or hunting crows' nests, both agreeable and exciting pastimes, but they were not for me. Wearing the look of one of the more bad-tempered martyrs, I crept down into the depths and resigned myself to my hard lot.

Potato plants had their special insect pest, the striped Colorado beetle. The Kremlin charged us with dropping potato bugs from airplanes on the fields of Soviet states. Uncle Joe didn't know his practical entomology. If you want potato bugs, all you need to do is to plant potatoes. Iron curtains mean nothing to *Doryphora decemlineata*. Though your garden is in the wilderness, the bugs will wear a path to your garden gate. The Soviets might try spraying with a solution of Paris green. If that doesn't stop the bugs, pick them off the vine and drop them in a can of kerosene. The surest way is to smash them between a couple of flat paddles. We tried all three methods, and still there were bugs. Perhaps the Russian experts can come up with something better, a bug bomb maybe.

Along with the potatoes there were a few rows of sweet corn, carrots, beets, radishes, lettuce, parsnips, onions, squash, usually sweet potatoes, beans, and peas. Our asparagus bed was a hardy perennial, seeming to take care of itself. Tomatoes there were of course. One of the few exotic delicacies that grew in our garden was a distant cousin of the tomato, known to us as the ground cherry. New England gardeners call it strawberry tomato. Whatever its proper name, this small yellowish fruit, enclosed in a protective husk resembling a Japanese lantern in shape, produces the most delicious jam that mortal man has yet tasted. The plant is hardy, easily grown, seeding itself lavishly, and the only known pests that afflict it are small children. Cocktail sippers regard it highly in the raw state, but its proper destiny is the jam closet.

One year I decided to launch out as a gardener on my own account, with dreams of a profitable cash crop, and I petitioned for a small strip of ground at the side of the working garden. There, for some mysterious reason, I planted Jerusalem artichokes, a very different article from the mildly entertaining ornament of discriminating tables. The Jerusalem brand grows tall and rank, resembling the sunflower, and mine were particularly rank. The root is supposed to be edible, but no one in the neighborhood seemed to find it so and I sadly fed them to the pigs. That was my sole youthful venture in independent gardening, if I omit the hill of peanuts that I grew in order to prove that it could be done in Illinois. The peanuts grew and blossomed according to schedule and I covered the blossoms with earth as instructed, but a fence-breaking pig found them and all that I had for proof was a few bits of shell. But I could boast that I was once a peanut grower.

It is clear that our vegetables were the standard varieties, with no time spent on the more exotic specimens or hybrids, salsify, soybeans, broccoli, or spinach. Vitamins were unknown and household debates over the relative merits of spinach and broccoli were far in the future. Farmers in our neighborhood took a dim view of salad, even lettuce. "Grass is for horses" was the general verdict, but I disagreed to the extent of a weakness for fresh crisp leaves of lettuce sprinkled with sugar. I still like it that way. Rhubarb plants were easy to grow and rhubarb pie, with plenty of sugar, was deservedly popular. In proof thereof we called it "pieplant," the name "rhubarb" being reserved for a particularly nauseating medicine for stomach disorders. In the corn belt the soybean now competes with corn for the place of honor, to the great benefit of the soil, but I doubt if the edible variety has yet found its way to many farm tables, and bean sprouts are still unknown.

We ate greens, but no spinach or chard. Ours were turnip tops or mustard leaves. Turnip leaves are given a high rating now for vitamin content, but they are still coarse in texture and in flavor. Young mustard leaves, with the stems eliminated, are pleasantly piquant, especially with meat juices added. Occasionally we made our own mustard, but our favorite condiment was horseradish made from roots grown in our garden and grated and mixed with vinegar of our own making. A slice of bread and butter spread thinly with horse-radish was an appetizing snack between meals.

While we did well with vegetables, perhaps a little above average, it was in fruit that we really shone. Our orchard had a considerable variety of apples, Red Astrachan, Siberian Crabs, Snow, Willowtwigs, Genitans, Bellflower among them. Father's sales resistance was high on most things, but he was helpless in the hands of a nursery salesman armed with an illustrated catalogue revealing a world in which all apples were large and round and rosy and peaches were really peaches. Every year a new variety crept in on us and some of them flourished. Most of the newer kinds are long since forgotten, but I do remember one, the Walbridge. When he planted this tree, Father produced a mnemonic formula for the name: "Think of the Great Wall of China and the Brooklyn Bridge and there you have it." Some of us remembered the formula, but forgot the reason for it. Fortunately the Walbridge died young.

The various apples had their special uses, apple butter, baking, pies, jelly. The Siberian Crab gave us a delicious jelly, clear amber in color, fruity in flavor, with a touch of tartness that indicated character. It was the Snow that we hailed as the "eating apple" par excellence. The flesh was white with a hint of pinkness through it, and one who has never tasted a Snow can hardly claim to have eaten an apple.

Our apple trees were mature and healthy, with no benefit of spraying in those pre-pest days, and a bumper crop was unfailing, barring a hard frost in blossom time. Again the sense of smell provokes memory, and a whiff of apple blossoms in early spring now will transport me to an earlier and a peaceful world.

In picking time small and misshapen specimens were put in special barrels, destined for vinegar by way of cider. Sweet cider, minus benzoate of soda, was a popular drink, but as it grew hard unexpected results might appear. In the give and take of local politics, Father had become a justice of the peace. His knowledge of the law was not profound; it didn't need to be. He knew the people among whom he had lived so long, and he had a keen sense of justice as a principle of life. Most of the cases were of the simplest kind, suits for the collection of debts, sometimes claims for damage caused by trespassing stock, disputes over the maintenance of a line fence between adjoining farms.

Once the disputants arrived at our house late in the afternoon, and our kitchen became a courtroom until early the next morning. A barrel of cider halfway on the road to vinegar had been left standing by a back gate. As the night wore on spectators were observed to tiptoe out of the room frequently and the legal tension was visibly lessened. It was low tide in the cider barrel when the trial ended, but it had been a pleasant battle and even the losers felt better than losers usually did.

Apples were our major fruit, but a double trellis of Concord grapes ran them a close second in season. The kitchen turned out quantities of grape jam and jelly, but my keenest recollection is of Concords fresh from the vine and still warm from the September sunshine. At the edge of the old town of Concord, Massachusetts, is a tablet commemorating the birth of the first Concord grape, produced by Ephraim Wales Bull. Many lesser men and things have bigger memorials but few that are more deserved.

We had one fruit not common in farm orchards in that time, damson plums, two trees of them. These were a sentimental gesture toward the English past. There had been damsons in Grandfather's garden in old Sussex, and jam and pies were made of them. So we had damson jam and pies. Eaten raw they lacked the juicy richness of other plums, but between flaky pie crusts they were a pleasure to meet.

Our supreme triumph in small fruit was strawberries, and our bed never failed us. At least that's the way I remember it. Strawberries must be ripe, but not too ripe, to be at their best. Then with rich country cream and plenty of sugar they left nothing to be desired. Shortcake was a compromise, acceptable only when the cake was biscuit and there was no economizing in the berries. Any other kind of shortcake is an abomination in the sight of all good judges of food.

Speaking of farm food, butchering time should not be overlooked. That was the ceremony that ushered in a feast of fresh meat. The victim was usually a hog, with now and then a calf or a fat steer, and the time was any winter day when the family larder needed refilling. It was a neighborhood affair, bringing in the services of a man or two with special skills in such gory occupation. The imported workers were rewarded with a share of the meat. Necessary equipment was a big iron kettle for heating water, a barrel big enough to slide the porker in for scalding away the hair, a strong table of rough boards for the cutting, an overhead support for the hanging of the carcass, and plenty of sharp butcher knives.

The successive steps in the process are omitted here, lest offense be given the tender susceptibilities of a generation that knows nothing of slaughtering, at least of slaughtering animals. A young man, normal, robust, with much experience in wilderness wandering, once spoke of his distatste for venison of his own killing, remarking that we would probably all be vegetarians if the alternative were the killing of our own meat. That gave me to think. Were we callous barbarians then? I can't believe it. We had to have meat and that was our way of getting it. Considering that man has been largely carnivorous for several thousand years, is there a better reason than hunger for killing our fellow animals? The true barbarism is the desire for a trophy to adorn the wall.

Consider the dietary possibilities of a single hog. First there were the obvious products: chops, roasts, spareribs. Spareribs are not convincing food to the inexperienced eye, something for the family dog perhaps, but can anyone mention meat that is sweeter or more tender? Almost it persuades me that sauerkraut is edible. Tender roast pork, not too dry, is both substantial and delicate. For me the top item on the butchering list was country sausage. We had it in abundance, made from our own pigs and flavored with sage of our own growing. It is still delectable on winter mornings, preferably with a long wandering in snow-covered woods to follow. My heart goes out to a half-starved generation that knows only frankfurters or liverwurst.

There were other incidentals that we owed to the pig, head cheese for example; we called it souse. If Philadelphia scrapple were less like fried mush and more like souse it might resemble souse. We ate it cold and in contrast with sausage I found it cheerless and of low repute. Pig's feet too found little favor in my sight, although with the years I have become more reconciled. Ham and bacon were of course the year-round reason for the pig, the meat staples we had always with us. Roast beef was for company or for threshers—usually overdone—fresh fish was a happy accident, but bacon and ham were the year-round reliables. When these failed famine was just around the corner. Fat pork cut in thick slices and fried to a golden brown is an amazingly sweet, appetizing dish. Try it some Saturday evening instead of cold ham with your weekly baked bean ceremonial, New England, and rejoice as we did!

Life being what it is, they had one drawback, these old reliables, that of lending themselves too readily to that curse of old-time country cooking, the frying pan. Makers of patent medicines owed much to it. Men stoking up for a long day in the open air, boys headed for school and the riotous play of recess, could work it off. It was the women tied indoors by household drudgery who were the chief sufferers and women were the mainstay of the proprietary tycoons. What a shock it would have been to respectable farm wives to learn that the relief they thought they felt was due largely to alcohol and cheap opiates!

In spite of the manner of its cooking, fried corn-meal mush was a welcome dish in our house. We grew the corn and had it ground in a local mill. There had been a time, not too long before, when Illinois was dotted with gristmills along small creeks of dependable flow. By my time only one of these remained in our neighborhood, Pete's on Cedar Creek, about ten miles away. The Minneapolis steampower giants had crowded out the others, but Pete hung on, with corn-meal his chief product. Draining the prairie lands had reduced the summer flow of our small streams to a mere trickle, and sometimes not even that, but seventy years ago Cedar and Henderson and Edwards held water for mills—and fish—the year round.

When a trip to Pete's mill could combine corn for grinding and a spot of fishing, one's cup of joy was full. It wasn't much as trout fishermen rate fishing, but it was the best we could do. Our fish was the humble cat, not highly regarded as a fighter, but with a half-pound cat on the hook and a fifty-pound boy on the butt end of a willow pole, there were moments of tension and thrill. Most of our cats ran a large shade under that weight, although the Mississippi sometimes delivered twenty-pounders to the commercial fisherman. Cleaned and broiled over an open fire as soon as possible after he came out of the water, the catfish had his points.

Corn meal served several purposes with us, corn bread of course, pancakes, and Indian pudding, too, after the manner of New England Saturday night suppers. Fried corn-meal mush has been mentioned with praise, but with cream and sugar, or better still butter and sugar, corn meal was, and is, an excellent cereal.

Fried mush and pancakes suggest syrup. Here again we grew our own. It seems to me that every year we found place for an acre or two of sorghum cane, a remote Chinese cousin to the sugar cane of the South. At a little distance a field of it resembled dwarf corn, without ears. The time for cutting the cane was in September, before the blades had begun to turn brown. The blades were stripped from the stalks, leaving the canes standing like so many slender poles. For cutting we used corn knives, somewhat like machetes, but much lighter. The seed tassels were cut away and the canes laid in small heaps between the rows, ready to be loaded on a wagon and hauled to the mill.

The sorghum mill I remember best was on the Clute farm a mile and a half away over a rough, hilly back road, nothing but a faint wagon track. There were many such roads built in the early hopeful days for the traffic that never came. The process of syrup making was a primitive forerunner of the great Cuban *centrales* of today, crushing the cane between rollers and boiling the sap in large flat pans. There was a bit of an art in judging the right stage for calling the job done, somewhere short of crystallization, but past the danger of fermentation. Don't ask me how it was done, partly the length of time, partly the look of it, partly the taste, probably some part luck. The boss kept the fire going and let the chemistry of nature take its course. The color was a bright amber, and the syrup was slightly viscous, with a distinct flavor of the cane. We knew the maple was more delicate, but maple trees were not common in Illinois and our soil was friendly to sorghum. The cost was a little land and labor and we had plenty of both.

It will be seen that we lived well. The land saw to that if we played fair with the land. Depressions came and went, the eighties were a decade of low prices for corn and hogs, money was scarce, and taxes and mortgages were insistent. Patches multiplied on our clothes, but we never had to tighten our belts in lieu of eating. There were always potatoes in the cellar, hams and bacon too, and salt pork in huge earthenware jars, apples in the bins through most of the winter, jams and jellies on the shelves. We canned few vegetables, but we did commit the minor atrocities of dried apples and corn. I suppose these were better than nothing, but in my book nothing ran them a close second.

In our daily living money was only an occasional incident. Ours was a self-sustaining economy. There was usually a surplus of potatoes, apples in season, eggs, and butter. It was with these that we paid for the "dry" groceries that were beyond the power of our land to produce. Our account with I. R. Green & Sons in Galesburg was on a barter basis. Books were balanced once a year and there was little to pay either way. This was subsistence farming as hundreds of farmers knew it, and here was our sure defense against depression, inflation, and the various chills and fevers that beset our economy. It was a slow way to wealth, but it sustained us on the road.

Our food supply was not limited to our gardens, orchards, and livestock. The woods around provided wild fruits, blackberries, crab apples, good for jelly if there was plenty of sweetening, the small wild grapes too tart for eating from the vine but with similar jelly possibilities, and plums, from which slightly astringent but flavorsome jam could be made. For winter evenings hickory nuts, walnuts, hazel nuts, butternuts—the Indian had known and used them all. Picking wild blackberries was a form of sport, taking us into clearings in thick timber and fence corners along the edges of old fields.

Being country boys we hunted and fished as a matter of course, although our game was on the small side. My specialty was rabbits, and killing rabbits came under the head of public service. If they were allowed to flourish unchecked they could easily become a pest in gardens and orchards.

While we were still at the gunless age dogs were our only means of catching up with the speedy cottontail. The figure-four traps that we whittled out so carefully were usually ignored. The boy plus dog technique was simple. In winter piles of slashings left by wood cutters were favorite hiding places for pesky cotton tails. I had a reliable dog named Dash, the same Dash that was allergic to wolves. He was a collection of several breeds, including a touch of greyhound, and rabbits were just his dish. Tramping a pile of brush brought the rabbit out full speed with Dash at his heels. Unless the underbrush was thick or the rabbit more than usually long-winded, a hundred yards or less told the story and the first boy on the spot pried Dash loose from the rumpled game. It wasn't very sporting, but when we hunted rabbits we were not concerned to give the game a chance. What we wanted was something for the pot.

A rabbit hunt was an invariable feature of our Christmas celebration. I am at a loss to explain the absence of any sort of religious observance of the day. There was no survival of the old Puritan belief among us, marking this day as a form of papistical idolatry. The Coldbrook church four miles away went in for Christmas trees on Christmas Eve, with candles and tinsel and gifts. Tylerville, even in more prosperous years, had no money to spend on such frivolity, and the giving of presents was not a universal practice. We did spread ourselves a little on the Christmas dinner, at least a plum pudding. Ours was the pudding of the English working man, sanctified by long custom: suet, raisins, and citron, boiled in a bag.

There was another local custom that involved rabbits in a festive occasion, this time an oyster supper. The connection of rabbits with oysters may not be obvious, but it was clear to us. The rabbits paid for the oysters. On an appointed day an elite corps of gunmen, self-appointed, took positions around a strip of brushy woodland known to be overcrowded with rabbits, and we, the gunless, came through the rabbity jungle, driving the game toward the firing squad. Sometimes the bag was large, fifty or more. These were traded to a local grocery store for the oysters to make the stew. Unfortunately I was violently allergic to that particular dish, the only food allergy that I have discovered in myself. In my memory of oyster suppers the thrill of the chase, if it could be called that, is clouded over by the gastronomic upheavel that followed the stew. In time I learned to take my oysters in some other form or leave them alone.

One winter we youngsters really struck pay dirt in our rabbit hunts. A stretch of cutover land grown up to scrub trees and hazel brush was usually good for a rabbit or two. The rabbit's burst of speed, plus his short wheel base, gave him a big advantage over even a clever dog, and this particular bit of cover gave us lots of running but little game. It was a hollow log that paid off for us. One winter the rabbits got into the unwise habit of making straight for this haven of refuge, leaving the dog scratching and raving helplessly outside. It was a situation to baffle a dog, but not a hungry boy. A long stick poked into one end of the hollow log sent the rabbit scurrying out the other, where he was scooped up by the guard at the back door, proper police procedure. It was a good trick while it lasted, which was only a season or two.

Incidentally, it was a rule of the household that whoever caught a rabbit should also dress it. That was no great hardship to us, inured as we were to butchering on the farm.

Bird shooting was not commonly practiced by the gunners of our family, although there were a good many quail in the fields and along the old fence rows. There were a few ruffed grouse in the woods—we called them pheasants—and as we roamed about, an occasional high velocity shell would explode at our feet and go zooming off through the trees. If one of us hit one of them as he sailed away, as Charlie did one day, with an old muzzle-loading rifle at that, the rest of us interpreted it as a sign that that particular bird's number was up and that if he hadn't been shot he would have broken his neck against a tree before the day was out. Charlie was a good rifle shot, but he wasn't that good.

Prairie chickens still lingered, but they were going fast and long before I was grown they had joined the passenger pigeon and the heath hen. It was the plow and not the gun that ended the day of this beautiful bird. When the last of the prairie grass was plowed under, Illinois was no longer a fit place for prairie chickens. In the Dakotas they lasted longer, but they are rare now anywhere. Immigrant birds have taken their place, Mongolian, Manchurian, British and Hungarian, sporting and beautiful, but not our own.

The law had little to say about seasons and bag limits in those primitive days, and a shooting license or a No Hunting sign would have been resented as an obvious encroachment on free enterprise. Take the case of wild ducks. The best time for duck shooting was during the spring flight, now a perpetual closed season. While the fall flight was on, corn picking monopolized our daylight hours, although city sports might indulge. Spring, too, was the time when there was plenty of water on the prairie lands, many of them still undrained, and the Henderson bottom only a mile from our house was a wide stretch of flood water. Those who took their duck shooting seriously had decoys and duck calls and hip boots, but that sort of outfit made roast duck too expensive for us. Shooting a duck on the water was plain common sense. Why add to the already heavy odds on the duck? My memory of youthful duck shooting is filled chiefly with long days, a few shots, wet feet, and a good time generally.

Wild geese dropped in on us occasionally, but few stayed permanently. They were too smart and shy for our small skill. The man who first used goose as a synonym for silly didn't know *Branta Canadensis*. Whoever got the better of one of them earned his roast goose. We saw few geese within shooting range, but we heard their call on rainy, windy nights in early spring. The sound of the honking dropping down to us, earthbound and helpless, had power to stir the most sluggish blood, and to have heard it once is to remember it forever. That was the authentic voice of wild America.

There were other seasonal reasons besides rabbits for wandering in our woods. For example, there were crows. The crow was a nuisance in the farmer's cornfields when the tender sprouts were beginning to trace faint lines of green across the black earth, and crows liked corn sprouts. A flock of crows could do almost as much to annoy the farmer as a late frost or a heavy hailstorm. Storms were acts of God, obscure and expensive, but beyond our power to avert or control. Crows were emissaries of the devil and we could do something about them. The time for crow hunting was in the early spring when the raucous demands of the young birds would lead the hunter to the nests. In our simple philosophy it was crows or corn, but all our hunting of the birds and wrecking of the nests had little visible effect on the supply of black brigands.

Crows are a canny people with a well-developed system of communication. Try to slip up on a flock engaged in uprooting a farmer's corn; long before you are in shotgun range, a sentinel sounds the alarm and the gang is in full flight. It was our firm belief that crows could count up to three. Hence if four men are in a field, and three leave, the crows assume that all have gone. At least that was our belief. I never saw it demonstrated and I never saw a foolish crow. We believed, too, that if one caught a crow young and split his tongue he could be taught to talk. I never saw that tested either, but I am certain that a talking crow would have spoken discreetly.

The most romantic and alluring of our sports was coon hunting. The time for it was in the fall when the fur was "set" and the night air held a hint of winter. Dan had a pack of hounds, as has been recorded, and coon hunting was his specialty. A few times I was permitted to go along, with stern warning that if I got separated from the others and had to spend the night in the woods, it was entirely my own affair. Unpleasant as that would have been, I accepted the risk cheerfully and never had reason for regret. Night in the woods was always a time of mystery and allurement to me, although I knew that home and a comfortable bed were only a few miles away. Woods, roads and paths, known and commonplace in the daylight, leading to familiar houses and barnyards, became trails leading to secret hiding places in a remote and tempting wilderness. North and south were meaningless terms. Noises in the darkness were strange and sometimes menacing. Moonlight filtering through the branches, making weird patterns of light and shade, increased the air of mystery.

As an enterprise, coon hunting produced more romance than coonskins, although Dan wore his coonskin coat with pride and comfort. In Illinois winters a coonskin coat was an article of utility and not a badge of collegiate plutocracy. My hunting nights added little to the season's catch, but they were worth all the bumps and bruises and scratches acquired in my blind fumbling through the darkness. My personal disappointment over a coonless night was slight and fleeting. This fascinating citizen of the woods was worth knowing. His wrinkled face, with its look of bewildered curiosity, his tiny feet like a baby's hands, his tail with its broad bands of dark fur, made him unique among our wild things. He did us little harm beyond a few ears of green corn, and that was a small price to pay for letting him live.

CHAPTER XII

We Did It Ourselves

THE LACK of money threw upon us the necessity of practicing many homely arts long since surrendered to the factory and the market. We did much of our own carpentering as a matter of course. The farmer who couldn't build his own henhouse or woodshed wasn't much of a farmer. The professional was called in for work requiring special skill, such as the building of new houses or barns, but even with these we were close to pioneer days. Barns "raisings" were occasions for neighborly cooperation. Frames were raised and pinned in place by sheer manpower in a surprisingly short time. Every farmer was a reasonably competent shingler and a painter of sorts. I was a small boy when our new house was built, but I was called in to help with the lathing. A boy of eight or nine who couldn't drive a nail had something wrong with his head. Environment is a thorough teacher and necessity a hard master.

A barn-raising called for high pressure in farm kitchens. Raisings were festivals borrowed from colonial New England, minus the hard cider, home-brewed ale, and New England rum that had so roused the ire of straitlaced Jonathan Edwards as he contemplated the eating and drinking that had punctuated the raising of his church at Northampton. We had our occasional drinkers, but drinking was not a social pastime with us.

Each farm, especially the older ones, had some kind of small-scale workshop as part of standard equipment. Father was prepared to make simple repairs of harness, soldering of kitchen tinware, occasional patching of work shoes, and of course all kinds

of rough painting. My brother-in-law Dan, who was more of a
pioneer at heart than most of us, built the cradle in which all his
numerous children were rocked, proving his amateur status by
attaching the rockers lengthwise instead of across. Child psychologists should be interested to learn that no unpleasant results were
noted. Our home-made household utensils were crude clumsy
affairs, lacking the sense of form and finish that has made old New
England chopping bowls collector's items in antique shops.

Several homely arts centered in the kitchen. Canning fruits
and vegetables, preserving, making pickles, jams, and jellies were
universal. Sweet corn and apples were dried by the simple process
of spreading them in the sun, covered by a strip of netting to keep
off the flies that were always with us in warm weather. Baking
bread and making butter were weekly tasks in all farmhouses, and
honorable ones, but this fact never reconciled me to the fate that
required me to stand by the old-fashioned churn and work the
dasher up and down until the butter came. An apron tied around
my middle gave the final touch of effeminacy. For home-made
bread I have only praise. Properly kneaded and raised by a warm
stove and baked in a slow oven, fresh bread still hot from the baking, liberally spread with butter and, if possible, honey was balm
for weary souls. Those who know only the commercial article,
highly recommended over the radio, have never eaten bread.

We made our own soap as well as our own bread, at least
enough for the weekly washday. The process was simple. Down
in the edge of the orchard stood a large, hopper-shaped wooden
bin in which wood ashes were deposited. As soap-making time approached, water was poured on the ashes and presently a trickle of
amber-colored liquid began to run down into a jar waiting for it.
This was lye, pure and powerful. The final stage was the boiling
in a huge iron kettle hung over an open fire. Fat meat scraps, saved
for the occasion, were dumped into the kettle, the lye added, and the
evil-smelling mixture boiled until the housewife decided that soap
had been accomplished. We used this soap only for washing work
clothes and scrubbing floors. It was too violently detergent for the
human skin, although for the real pioneers the choice was this

kind of soap or nothing. Quite a number chose nothing. My only contribution to the making of soap was keeping the fire going under the kettle, a leisurely and alluring occupation, remotely akin to building a campfire.

There was the matter of tallow candles. My youth fell in the long period between whale oil and electricity. Kerosene was standard for lamps and lanterns, but kerosene cost money and was to be used sparingly. Besides, a lighted kerosene lamp was a tricky thing to carry about the house. Candles were indicated for casual uses. Our own were made in tin moulds, six at a time. The melted tallow, also home produced, was poured into the moulds, where the wicks had been inserted, and the job hung up to cool and harden. Then the finished candles were lifted out and laid away in the pantry. Candles are still with us, but not as everyday utilities, merely the finishing touch on the well-dressed dinner table. And they are not made of tallow. The candle made of wax has become a symbol of a luxury-loving and helpless age.

It will be noted that the life of a farm wife was no picnic. Consider the case of my mother with her family of four sons and two daughters, born over a stretch of fifteen years. To be sure I recall no time when we were all living at home at the same time, but even so we were something of a housefull. In addition to the cooking, baking, canning, preserving, soap and candle making, there was sewing, knitting, patching, washing, ironing, and the added pressure with threshers or not infrequent guests for Sunday dinner. Our house was without inside plumbing, refrigeration, or central heat. Farm kitchens were always hot in summer when the pressure was greatest. As income improved, a few simple mechanical appliances were added to our primitive equipment, an apple parer, a sewing machine, a meat grinder, but no washing machines, dishwashers, inside incinerators, or deep freeze, none of the conveniences that make the modern kitchen the most attractive room in the house. My memory holds no picture of my mother sitting with folded hands. An observer looking in on us in the sitting room of a winter evening would have seen Father nodding over the local paper, spectacles slipping down on his nose, me in my favorite place prone behind the warm stove reading, Mother in her rocking chair eternally knitting or sewing. Except in cold weather the kitchen was the family center. There we cooked, ate, lived, and had our being.

Blacksmithing had moved from the individual farm to the local shop, but the art practiced there was still of the crude variety familiar to the pioneers, shoeing horses, setting wagon tires, simple welding of broken tools. Equipment was equally simple, a forge with hand or foot bellows, an anvil, a rough bench with a vise, and a meager assortment of hammers, tongs, and wrenches. Many of the older farmers could manage a rough equivalent of the blacksmith's job if the regular smith was busy with another customer, or maybe chasing a catfish down on Henderson Creek.

Now the old blacksmith has gone on down the road to oblivion and the garage mechanic has taken his place, but the garage cannot replace the old shop as a loafing place and a center for the exchange of local gossip and the display of political wisdom in campaign time. Jerry Hawkins ran just such a shop across the road from our house. That was our favorite rendezvous on rainy days, especially when an unruly horse required shoeing.

Where Jerry learned his trade was one of the neighborhood mysteries, the general opinion being that he hadn't learned it anywhere, he just did it. Later on he added a small gristmill for the grinding of corn in a shed near-by. It was literally a one-horse mill and when I could slip away from the house unobserved I was often the driver of the horse. Jerry rewarded me occasionally with a small piece of change when he had it, which wasn't often, but my real compensation was being a part of a commercial enterprise.

Jerry's leaky shed was far from the village smithy that Longfellow immortalized, but even that cluttered smoky interior hinted dimly of romance, at least in retrospect. It was alluring, the flames leaping on the forge, sparks showering from the anvil, the smell of hot iron, the sound of rain beating on the roof, the idle, frequently bawdy talk of Jerry and the loafers standing by.

Mrs. Jerry practiced another old craft, the weaving of rag carpets. There was scarcely room to move about in the two rooms and shed leanto of her shabby home, but somehow she found space for her loom. Her customers were the farm wives of the neighborhood. Old dresses, shirts, aprons, anything that had passed beyond the darning and patching stage, furnished material for the woof. Rainy days and winter evenings were good times for tearing these remnants into narrow strips. When enough were accumulated for a strip of carpet, Mrs. Jerry had another order. Most of us had no other covering for our floors. Even the cheapest rugs and carpets that the local store offered were luxuries. When carpets were to be had as by-products of our old clothes, why dream of luxuries?

Another by-product of our wardrobes was quilts. In our neighborhood no family was without them. Quilting called for cooperative work, and gossip could pass freely around the quilting frame. Mother, who talked little and never gossiped, regarded community quilting with little favor, but needing quilts she endured the party. Every wife had her own treasured patterns, Rising Sun, Log Cabin, Old Maid's Puzzle, Bear's Paw, Wedding Ring, Sunburst, names that suggest bits of folklore buried deep in a forgotten past. The quilts were records of family wardrobes—a bit of Molly's old blue dress that she never liked, a dash of Charlie's favorite red shirt, a strip of that terrible checked suit that Phil has been permitted to choose. Items of our family treasures today are two quilts salvaged from that old life, still useful and still beautiful.

Home tanning had gone out with the disappearance of deer, and cowhides were scraped and dried in the sun and sold to a local dealer. Phil made one experimental return to the day of buckskin clothing. Inspired by a deer-hunting trip with Dan in the swamps of Mississippi he came back with enough buckskin for a pair of pants, which he proceeded to make. Painfully copying an old cloth pair of his own he cut and stitched through many patient evenings. The result was not impressive in fit or style, but they were clearly buckskin pants, complete to the fringe down the legs. After a wetting they came out of the drying shrunken and stiff as boards, but he wore them proudly when he rode with Dan in a wolf chase. The rest of us stuck to overalls.

Another local enterprise was brickmaking and the production

of tile for the draining of wet fields. Our brickmaker was Hank Miles. If it had not been for the discovery of a bed of clay suited for bricks in a corner of hilly pastureland, Hank would have been just another farmer with a knack for mechanical things. I suppose his farmer customers groaned over the prices as they fumbled in their shrunken wallets, but at least they dealt directly with the maker, without intervention of wholesalers, brokers, or retailers. The buyer provided his own transportation.

I have spoken of tile for draining fields. This simple, useful article was an agency in the creation of one of our pressing problems in our chief breadbasket, the drainage basin of the Mississippi and its confluents. To the farmer, fields where water stood through the plowing season were a clear loss, and the tile drain was the answer to his prayers. As with so many other human improvements, the unseen and unwanted results went far toward outweighing the gain. In the wet season the drains ran full, sending the water down the little capillaries to merge with other trickles into larger streams and finally into the great river itself. The farmer's fields dried early and he rejoiced as he plowed. The fact that there were floods and broken levees downriver was nothing to him. Leagues of prairie land that had stood waist deep in grass since the last glacier died were now green with corn.

During the first World War the slogan "Food will win the war" brought to the farmer the illusion of unending and unlimited wealth. Prices were high and going higher. The cry was for more land to plow and bigger crops. A new thing now appeared in the land, a strange combination of farming, local government, and high finance, called a Drainage District. Swamps along the rivers were drained and fenced with levees, bonds were sold to people who never held the handles of a plow or picked a bushel of corn, and more people shared the golden dream. No thought was given to the obvious fact that these swamps were holding reservoirs for excess water at flood time, slowing down the runoff and reducing the volume in the main channels pushing toward the Gulf of Mexico. The awakening came when gangs of workers patrolled the levees day and night to spot the threatened breaks and rush sandbags there to save the district. Evidently the high gods viewed Drainage Districts with disfavor. Man interferes with the balance of nature at his peril. Some of the districts came through alive, others went back to the frogs and the fish and the wild ducks.

Farther north the great forests of pine came downriver as rafts of logs and lumber, and the lumber barons rejoiced and counted their profits. With the destruction of the grass and the forest cover, the land lay naked under the sun and rain, and melting snow hurried off to join the rush to the Gulf. Fertile topsoil went along with the flood waters, but we were in too much of a hurry to count the ultimate costs. Now the dwellers along the Mississippi, the Ohio, the Illinois, the Missouri, and lesser streams fight floods every spring and curse the elements that have brought disaster to them. The M.V.A., if there is ever an M.V.A. to match the T.V.A., should have a drainage tile marked with a bar sinister on its coat of arms. The horse has been stolen and the stable door is hard to lock, but we should at least remember that it was we who left the door open to the thief.

The barter system, payment in goods or labor for other goods or services, extended even to certain kinds of taxes. Our roads were crude affairs, wagon tracks between farm fences, unbelievably bad in bad weather, innocent of gravel or other hard surface; but good or bad we made them and kept them at least passable most of the year. Part of our year's program was so many days' work on the roads to pay our road taxes, measured in the usual terms of man and horse time. The township owned the simple road-working machinery of scrapers and graders, but we provided the men, the horses, and the time. A "pathmaster," merely another farmer elected by us in each school district, directed the work more or less, but each farmer usually put in his time on the stretch of road most important to him.

Our method of road-working was simple, little more than dragging the dirt from the side of the road to the middle, filling in the worst mudholes, and gradually easing the grade of the steeper hills. We built the smaller bridges that called for nothing more than a board culvert covered with earth or a couple of sleepers across a stream with two-inch planks nailed to them. Larger bridges involving piles and approaches were contract jobs for the township or county.

I got in on one of those contract jobs once. My brother Phil was road commissioner for the township, and when school was out he gave me a job hauling dirt from the top of a longish hill to build up the grade across the creek bottom below. The wage was two-fifty a day for man and team. It was a soft snap for me. The home farm furnished the team and wagon and all I had to do was to sit on the front end of the wagon and draw my two-fifty per diem. It lasted only a week or two, but I came out of it with a new suit of clothes bought with my earnings.

A stretch of road newly worked could be a snare and a delusion in wet weather. Wagons sank to the hub in the loose earth heaped in the center, and deep ruts made travel an extra-hazardous undertaking. What they were like when heavy rain was followed by a sharp freeze cannot be described. Most of our roads took no account of contour lines or grades but ran due north and south or east and west. Hills might be steep but they were short, and we went straight up and over. Bad as they were sometimes and straight as they were all the time, the old country roads had a charm that the arterial highway for all its parking and landscaping cannot hope to rival. The wagon tracks ambled leisurely along between the fences, skirting mudholes, over little hills, across small streams, through stretches of shady woodland, a natural part of the landscape, more definite than a trail but less domineering than a ribbon of concrete. We had no speed limits, the roads took care of that. Our errands seldom took us more than two or three miles from home, and if we could get there and back without too much discomfort and delay it was enough.

We had our specialists in homely arts, the result of a knack plus experience rather than training. One of our neighbors was much in demand at butchering time, although the highly skilled—and highly paid—meat cutters of today would dismiss him as a bungler. At least he knew where the best cuts were and how to get them out without waste or delay. Dave Terpening loved his orchard more than his fields and his trees were local miracles of budding and grafting. All women were cooks and dressmakers, but some were better than others. When I went away to school to prepare for college all the shirts in my slender wardrobe were home-made.

Children were born with the aid of one of the older women near-by, frequently without benefit of doctor or nurse. Many families viewed doctors with suspicion, to be sent for only as a last resort. If the doctor came for a maternity case he could be sure that he would find an amateur midwife there before him. Aunt Mary Adcock, Dan's mother, was one of the reliable amateur nurses, quick of foot and deft of hand whatever the illness, untiring and un-failing. In consequence she knew the ages of all of us, and no belle beginning to lose her luster could claim a tender age that was hers no longer. No night was too dark and no road too bad for Aunt Mary when the call came.

Our nearest veterinary was a dozen miles away and our sick or injured animals must do the best they could with what we had. Hank and George Adcock were brothers and neighbors who dif-fered radically over the proper treatment for hog cholera, a fre-quent scourge among us. Hank had a weakness for highly adver-tised remedies while George preferred to wait for the plague to wear itself out. When Hank announced that he had found the sure cure and that his hogs had proved it by getting well, George dis-missed the claim with profane scorn. "Your damned hogs just got ready to quit dyin', that's all."

Our practice of self-help covered the whole course of life from the cradle to the grave. We were born with local aid, we could be married by a country justice of the peace, and neighbors dug our graves. If desired there were one or two old-timers who could be counted on to preach the funeral sermon and say the last prayer. One of the local amateur parsons, unable to find the passage he wanted in the Book, was alleged by the irreverent to have inquired in a plaintive stage whisper, "Where is that damned text anyway?"

It was part of our country code that the learned professions were not so very learned and that those who practiced them were not to be regarded seriously as workers. Doctors were not quite such complete parasites as teachers and preachers, but they were seldom worth what they cost. A patient reminded Doc Hatchet that the dollar charged for an office call lasting only fifteen minutes would pay a man's wages for a day. When the doctor mentioned the time and money he had spent for his education the patient demanded, "Why should I pay for your education?" This to the neighbors was not only good repartee but sound sense. Besides, the sick man would have got well anyway. Most sick people did get well sooner or later, if they didn't die. Fractures, serious cuts, major illnesses like diphtheria or typhoid called for the services of a doctor. We knew nothing of specialists in medicine. The practice of the country doctor covered the whole range of human ailments and mishaps, and far too often we called him too late. Hospitals were unknown to us. Operations were dreaded and postponed or avoided if possible.

The worst feature of this attitude was the neglect of the health of children. Little attention was paid to the need for special diet, and malnutrition in the early years was common. A dentist was visited only when the pain of an aching tooth was no longer bearable. Such a thing as the preventive care of the teeth of children was unknown by both dentists and parents in our part of the country, and it was a matter of course that old people had false teeth or none at all. By the same token, weak eyes were the will of God, and when spectacles were necessary they were likely to be bought from pedlars whose knowledge of optometry was nil. When spectacles were accepted as inevitable, the first pair was expected to last from then on.

A moneyless economy had its advantages, in retrospect at least. Ours was not easily jarred by storms that knocked the money-changers about, although mortgages were always a source of worry. Small-town bankers were sympathetic and understanding of the farmer's problems and foreclosures were few in our township, even in the hard years of the early nineties. Since we produced our own food we were not likely to go hungry even when millhands walked the streets looking for work and stood in line for soup and a slice of bread.

CHAPTER XIII

Manners And Morals

I T IS a favorite American thesis that the frontier was the abode of such sturdy virtues as industry, thrift, rough and ready justice, all the cardinal essentials to right living. It was a time and place where men were men—and presumably—women were women. On the latter point there can be no doubt. Ours was not the frontier, only a fading echo of it, but the manness of men and the womanness of women were marked in both work and play.

Horses were in the man's half of the world. I knew only two or three girls who learned to ride, one of them my sister Molly, after she became a country school-teacher. They rode only from necessity, never for pleasure. Sidesaddles and long, cumbersome skirts were mandatory and a girl in riding breeches riding astride would have been a social pariah. We were aware that women had legs and our curiosity about them was at least normal, but women's legs were never mentioned in mixed company and for the owner of the legs to reveal them deliberately would have been cause for horrified or leering gossip. Clearly such a one was no better than she should be and that wasn't nearly good enough. Bathing suits offered no problem because women never swam. I doubt if there was a farm woman or girl in the whole county who knew how.

Women might drive a stolid old horse hitched to a top buggy, but I have no recollection of seeing a woman drive a team, certainly not in the field. Of course they never worked in the field, with or without horses, although wielding a hoe in the garden was permissible, in some cases necessary if there was to be a garden. Women

were not supposed to have any knowledge of the care of horses beyond the simple acts of harnessing and unharnessing, and that
only when there was no man available. The concept of woman had
no place for horsemanship.

There were similar dividing lines in play. Boys and girls
played together in recess time at school, but only in the earlier
years. Adolescence drew a sharp line and beyond this point the
girls disappeared from the ball games and the boisterous pum-
pum-pullaway. One husky Irish girl got herself talked about
around the district by playing baseball at the age of sixteen, and her
offense was the greater because she was a better player than most
of the boys. Clearly she could come to no good end. If she still
lives she is undoubtedly several times a grandmother and probably
critical of the unwomanly behavior of the modern girl.

Of course, we knew about sex. A boy on the farm learned the
facts of life early. It was impossible to live in the midst of domestic
animals without becoming aware of the basic biological urge. The
breeding of animals was a commonplace necessity if the flock or
herd was to be replenished. Roadside trees and fence posts carried posters announcing that a pure-bred Percheron or Norman
stallion was available at a certain farm and at a stated fee for
service. "Standing" was the country term for it. But the breeding
of stock was matter for the talk of men only. In mixed company the
subject was never referred to .

There were curious avoidances of words when a definite
designation of sex was necessary. "Bull" was barely permissible,
but I have heard a bull called a "male cow," which is some sort of
record in prudery. Such words as "stud" and "boar" were barred
and "bitch" was unthinkable, but "rooster" was a matter of course.
The convention required that only the most oblique and veiled
reference be made to an expected baby. Pregnancy was such a
guilty secret that the word was never mentioned.

It was the natural corollary of this morbid prudishness that
the conversation of men was flavored with coarse allusions to sex,
but this was seldom a fault with the older and more settled men of
the community. Itinerant farm workers were the worst offenders.

These gentry seemed to take a particular delight in shocking a sensitive boy with bawdy yarns that were without point or humor. One young man of the neighborhood had a collection of such tales which he would unfold with or without provocation. Later on he became a pillar of the church and censor of local morals, a not illogical transition.

I recall no instance of an older man talking seriously with a youngster about the nature and pitfalls of sex. The most careful and understanding explanation by a teacher as a legitimate part of the process of education would have brought instant dismissal. The natural result of this system of avoidance on the one hand and leering allusion on the other was to stimulate a boy's curiosity without warning him of the dangers ahead. We learned about sex in the worst way possible. Harm was done, and the fact that it was not greater can be credited to our native timidity and perhaps an innate sense of decency. Even so the atmosphere surrounding sex was unhealthy when it might so easily have been clean and decent. Those who object to adequate teaching of the facts of life as a smirching of the innocence of youth are talking about something that didn't exist in our neighborhood. Whatever else we were, we were not innocent on this point at least.

In principle the code of virtue was high and permitted no exceptions. Illegitimacy was neither forgiven nor forgotten. Even though the identity of the father was rather more than suspect, it was on the mother and the child that the penalty fell of course.

How well did this sort of social policing control the relations of the young before marriage? No one knows. When a young couple had reached the stage that we called "going together" there were occasional sly allusions to top buggies standing long on secluded side roads on summer evenings.

The ratio of domestic fidelity was high. Separations were infrequent and divorce practically unknown. The cost of such an extreme step was enough to discourage thought of it. Even today real farmers or farmers' wives are strangers to Reno. It should not be concluded that all marriages were happy ones, but in spite of frequent minor jangles home life was placid, though undemonstrative. Open expressions of affection were not common. Within the family circle kissing was for babies or the brief period of courtship. Our life was as sparing of praise as of money. Undoubtedly parents liked to hear their children praised, but the common response was deprecatory. Compliments were likely to make a child "big-headed." Also there was a lingering fear that praise of children to their faces was likely to attract the jealous attention of a bad-tempered God. One of my teachers incautiously in my presence told Mother that I was doing good work in school. The prompt reply was calculated to put me in my place: "He ought to. He's lazy enough at home." It didn't take us long to discover that this was a mere formality, part of a masquerade, not to be taken seriously. Like the whippings it was for our good, and like the whippings it had little effect.

Another virtue was industry. This we practiced almost without exception. We worked in order that we might eat and have a roof over our heads. We were proud of the fact that we were a law-abiding people, and in general we were. We paid our debts and we kept the peace. Petty thievery was rare, mostly such things as apples or watermelons. A special code had grown up around watermelons, amounting to tacit and usually good-natured warfare between the grower and the half-grown boys of the neighborhood. Melon patches were located with special reference to secrecy, in the middle of a cornfield or near the house, where a light sleeper might take warning of the progress of a raid. If you were caught nothing much happened except an irate dressing down to deepen the humiliation of failure. Even the marauders had a code of behavior. It was a serious irregularity to test the ripeness of a melon by cutting a sample plug out of it. If you couldn't pick a ripe melon in the dark by thumping it you were advised to stay honest.

The code that governed the personal relations of grown men was casual and tacit. Boys fought for any reason, or none at all. A spark of temper might turn a good-natured scuffle into a brawl with a wild flurry of futile blows. My first battle occurred before my conscious memory had begun to record events, so I have only family rumor to rely on. My opponent was one Freddy Richardson, otherwise unknown to me. I had been ordered to conduct Freddy to the strawberry bed and there to help him pick some berries to take home to his mother. A reference by the visitor to the fact that the berries were for him aroused my wrath, and we fell to in the midst of the berries, to the indignant shame of my mother and the vast amusement of Freddy's father.

With grown men there were a few words that called for instant action. The lie direct was not to be overlooked. Terms that demanded prompt physical retort were "bastard" and "son of a bitch." These were not to be used lightly or condoned if used.

Our social manners were simple but definite. Teachers and older people were addressed as "sir" or "Ma'am," as the case might be. In the vernacular an introduction was a "knockdown," and popular forms were "Miss Smith, meet Mr. Jones," or "Mr. Brown, shake hands with Mr. Robinson." If a name was not clearly understood, it was standard practice to inquire, "What's the name, please?" To one who has suffered much from strange names mumbled or jumbled in transmission it seems a sensible practice.

We had little skill in expressing gratitude or conveying compliments. If a young man had so far lost his head as to praise a young lady's hat or gown, both of them would have suffered torments of embarrassment. Doubtless there were exceptions, but I do not recall them. We had no skill in graceful phrases and well-turned compliments and we were wise to avoid them. Mother had a verdict of contempt for such insinuating advances; they were "blarney" and of doubtful taste.

Strangers coming among us found us indifferent, if not hostile. If the new family contained a good-looking daughter or son, adjustment was soon accomplished. Small boys might require some working over at recess on the school playground before they were admitted to full membership. If a newcomer spoke with a foreign accent, so much the worse for him. All outsiders were alien and a foreigner was doubly so. His knowledge of a foreign tongue was a count against him. Why didn't he speak English, as all decent people did? The story of the Englishman who rejected with scorn the French word for bread would have been appreciated by us. Why call it *pain* when everyone knew it was *bread?* The best that the unhappy foreigner could hope for his stumbling attempts at English was good-natured derision. How long has it been since an alleged Swedish dialect was sure-fire for a vaudeville comedian?

The line between city and country people was sharply drawn. The easy speech and the good clothes of the city men who came among us was reason enough for fearing the worst. The villain was easily identified in the melodrama of that day. He wore a silk hat, a frock coat, and sharp-toed patent leather shoes, and he smoked cigarettes. Give him a cane to swing nonchalantly, and the simple country maiden in a gingham dress hadn't a chance in the world.

Our clannishness in the presence of outsiders was a frontier heritage. In spite of the growth of population and the steady flowing of the American people westward for new land and another chance, there were backwaters like ours where time seemed to stand still. We were hundred per cent Americans, if there have been any, and we instinctively shied away from strange faces and new things. Our physical environment of woods and hills strengthened the illusion of permanence. Such youthful hoodlumism as we exhibited was possible because there were woods to roam in and hills to hedge us about. A dark night, country roads, and horses to ride stirred the pulse and called us to mischief. It was seldom malicious and it had no sinister meaning for the future. The boys who had fancied themselves as night riders soon settled down to respectable matrimony and hard work.

Many of the real bad men of the Old West were town products. Billy the Kid was born on the East Side in New York, and Wild Bill Hickok came from a small town along the Illinois. Most of his killing had warrant of law. Wyatt Earp and his brothers who tamed the killers in the corral fight in Tombstone grew up in Monmouth, our county seat town. They also were town marshals and deputy sheriffs, agents of law and order. The line between law enforcement and law breaking was a vague one. We may sometimes have seemed to flout the law, but our offenses were products of the time and place, with little significance except as the overflowings of youth and high spirits.

In spite of farm duties and long hours of work, there was no lack of social life. At the core of it was neighborly visitation, with Sunday dinner as an important feature. This was something of a feast, especially if the visiting wife was known to be a star in her own kitchen. If there was china and silver that could be described as "best," it was brought forth for such occasions. Children were included as a matter of course, and there was a nice question of age involved in determining the exact point at which this inclusion ceased to be automatic. Summer was preferred for these affairs. There was plenty of room out of doors for the young fry, although noisy play was frowned upon.

The sedate elders generally adjourned to the sitting room, commonly called the Best Room, after the hearty dinner had been duly dealt with. If the weather was bad, these Sunday afternoons were ordeals for the young, unless a roomy barn offered large opportunity for play. With the elders, talk drifted idly along obvious channels: the condition of crops, the price of hogs, the latest report from neigbborhood invalids—with much shaking of gloomy heads—politics always, if it was campaign time with party lines to attack or defend, religion sometimes, although this was a dangerous theme calculated to lead to violent dogmatic differences. The women discussed children and recipes and exchanged patterns for clothes or quilts. The family photograph album was good for half an hour or more any time. The routine of viewing the album never varied. "That's Roy when he was two. Wasn't he cute? Here's Aunt Martha when she was little. Would you ever believe it?" Aunt Martha also looks incredulous. Fortunately for all concerned, the album act has gone out—or has it?

The other Britt family, Uncle Jim and Aunt Martha, lived only half a mile away and a family dinner was indicated once or twice a year. These were far from being lively affairs. Mother's relations with her sister-in-law were in general those of a state of watchful neutrality. Aunt Martha's tongue was active and often sharp, and Mother held to the theory that she seldom regretted what she had never said. These contrasting traits made communication between them one-sided and unsatisfactory, but Aunt Martha had one approach that always struck sparks. On her one trip to London she had seen Queen Victoria ride by in her carriage of state, and invariably the queen appeared in the after-dinner talk, always to Mother's visible annoyance. "I never saw the queen," she would say tartly, and Aunt Martha unvaryingly replied, "Why, Sallie, didn't you?" in a tone of mingled surprise and superiority. To be called Sallie was offense enough, and the exchange never failed to leave a mark.

Uncle Jim was slow in speech and hesitant in manner, as though a little bewildered by the size and complexity of this American world. In accent he was still a piece of old country Sussex. To the end of his life February was Febivary as it had been in his youth. I remember mostly his gentle kindness to me, and the homemade jam with which Aunt Martha smeared a slice of fresh bread and country butter whenever I "happened" in.

Aunt Martha's favorite reading matter was newspaper reports of major catastrophes, fire or wreck or battle. The ghastly railroad crash at Ashtabula[1] must have kept her in good spirits for days, but that failed to impress me, except as an illustration of the sort of thing adults talked about. The same verdict goes for Aunt Martha's "best room." This might have been a museum piece straight out of Sussex planted in an Illinois farmhouse. By no stretch of the imagination could it be called a "sitting room." He who dared to step off the newspapers spread on the rugs was a rash fool, and to sit on one of the spindle-legged chairs was unthinkable. In the exact center was a small marble-topped table loaded with various objects ornamental in intent: artificial flowers, a small music box, never used, a photograph album, a Church of England prayerbook, each article always and forever in the same spot. In one corner of the room was a familiar piece of furniture called a "whatnot," its three shelves filled with small curios: a miniature pagoda built of shells glued together, an artificial bird perched

[1]On December 29, 1876, a train went through a flimsy wooden bridge at Ashtabula, Ohio, killing ninety-two people.

on an artificial twig, various small pieces presumably having some vaguely sentimental value, the sort of things sold at seaside resorts as souvenirs.

On the walls hung two or three pictures combining decorative and inspirational appeal, such as a storm-tossed figure clinging to the Rock of Ages in an angry sea. There was one that I recall with a sense of pathos. In a frame was a small lock of hair tied with a narrow ribbon. This was a sad reminder of the daughter who died so young and so long ago. It was without name or date, only that tiny blond curl, but it may have been that which gave the room the quality of a shrine heightened by the perpetual twilight of drawn shades so that even in the middle of a day in August a chill seemed to hover in the dark corners.

As in most farmhouses the kitchen was the family center, a small cosy place filled with delicious odors, preserves in the making, pies hot from the oven, fresh bread, all the homely fragrance of a working home. That other room may have been a shrine, but this kitchen embodied the kind of worship that a small boy could understand.

In his talk with adults there were two subjects that moved Uncle Jim to positive and occasionally belligerent argument, the iniquities of banks in general and those of Wall Street in particular and the superior efficacy of baptism by immersion. Father agreed with him in general on Wall Street, but he was still too much of an Anglican to accept immersion as a necessary means of salvation. The pattern of their casual talk after a heavy Sunday dinner was as fixed as the precession of the Equinoxes. The opening themes were merely prefatory, the weather, crop prospects, news from the Old Country, the chance for some old resident to pull through another winter—but these were merely ceremonial sparrings.

Whatever the subject touched, the talk moved inevitably to the proper technique for achieving salvation. This was serious, outside the realm of idle talk. Carefully chosen texts flew back and forth. What was the function of baptism in the time of John the Baptist? What form did he employ? Baptism was the word round which the war of words and texts whirled. Tempers grew warm and voices rose, until Mother or Aunt Martha announced that it was time to be thinking of home, where the chores were waiting. Naturally we youngsters steered wide of these sessions.

It would be unfair to label such a habit a quaint sample of old bigotry and narrowness. It was much more than that. To the disputants there was deep and lifelong faith behind the symbols. These men believed that man's spiritual destiny was important. The power and the love of God were real to them, ever-present forces in man's life. If we in our superior knowledge and deeper understanding have discarded dogma because we have lost our faith—and our courage with it—have we gained so much? The forms of their faith were simple because their lives were simple.

Sunday was a day of rest for older people, and the place to rest was a comfortable chair indoors. Only extreme heat could drive chairs and sitters outside to soft grass and the shade of convenient trees. After I had become an urban personage, inclined to view a walk in the woods or about the fields as a form of recreation, my divorce from the farm was complete. Fields and woods were for work and not for idle rambling by grown people.

Even mild games were held to be beneath the dignity of adults, although croquet was permissible if the house lot had suitable space and surface. Tennis was unknown to us, although it was creeping into the towns. There was one exception in the case of tennis. Bill Adcock, a prosperous farmer, liked what he heard about this game and came home from town one day bearing a full set of the necessary equipment, net, racquets, and balls. Dan saw it in operation and was moved to envy, but not to the extent of cash outlay for tools. A seine for fishing, which incidentally he had tied himself, was a fair net and he could make his own racquets, which he did, wooden paddles of at least the right shape and size. Balls of course were beyond him and called for cash. The resultant game was a burlesque of lawn tennis, even as it was played in that early day. But Dan had an idea. Paddle tennis is with us today and a a real game it is with no resemblance to pat ball.

Of course, being good Americans, we played baseball, but no games on Sunday, although batting and fielding practice could be

or the inflation of the big bag to the moment when the daring
eronaut cut loose with his parachute and floated down, usually
o land in the middle of a cornfield half a mile away. Hot-air bal-
oons had low ceilings so we had a good view of whatever happened.

For country people the fair was another and bigger picnic
with fried chicken, lemon pie, and endless visiting. Farmers from
all over the county met and gossiped around the pens of fat Chester
Whites or prize-winning Shorthorns, and women made envious
comment on the blue-ribbon peaches or the excellence of a patchwork quilt that the judges had ignored. There were exhibits of
work done in country schools. One year our district walked off
with some kind of a ribbon. The reason for our achievement is
forgotten, but it is certain that samples of my penmanship were
not included in the exhibit.

Picnics and baseball games were public affairs, open to all
comers. All that was needed was a festival mood and a basket of
lunch, and there were few who could not meet these simple requirements. "Parties" were more exclusive. Invitations, though usually
verbal, were necessary. Houses were small and space was limited,
so party crashing was looked upon with great disfavor. For entertainment we played parlor games, charades, post office, forfeits,
mild substitutes for the forbidden dance. Some of the games were
hard to distinguish from dancing, "Skip-cum-a-loo" for example,
with its chanted refrain, "I've got another girl, prettier than you,
Skip-cum-a-loo, my darling."

Many of them were kissing games. In post office the charge
for the delivery of a letter was a kiss. In forfeits the phrase ran,
"Heavy, heavy, what hangs over your head?" The victim must
inquire, "Fine or superfine?" "Fine" was for a man, "superfine"
for a girl. If the hidden article was loaned by a man, a favorite
penalty was "Speak to the prettiest, bow to the wittiest, and kiss the
one you love the best." Applause was always loudest for the gallant
youth who paid the tribute of the word, the bow, and the kiss to
the same girl. One quick-witted boy with many girl friends raised
a storm of protest by selecting his good-looking young mother. He
probably dodged a lot of trouble too.

indulged in. Horseshoe pitching was common and every farm had
a miscellaneous collection of old horseshoes hanging in the barn.
Neighborhood baseball rose and fell as the number of active young
men varied. There were two or three seasons when we Tylerville
players thought rather well of ourselves due to the appearance of a
young farmer nearby who could manage a backbreaking out-curve
and an unpredictable in. Unfortunately his control ranged from
uncertain to ultimate zero and our dream of a township champion-
ship never got to first base.

Diamonds were improvised wherever there was a large enough
stretch of level pastureland to give the players at least a chance to
field the ball, although I remember one where a long hit into right
field had a better than even chance of rolling down a slope into a
marshy creek at the bottom. There were bitter arguments over
the scoring of such a hit between the advocates of the theory that a
hit was a hit and those who held to the limited liability concept that
such a performance was an act of God and not a home run. Umpires
if any, generally followed the rule of safety first by balancing an
outrageously wrong decision in favor of team *A* by an equally absurd error in behalf of team *B* at the first opportunity. There were
few pitchers' battles and scorers were kept busy. Thirty-two to
twenty-five was regarded as a close game and entirely satisfactory
to the spectators.

A small coal-mining community ten or fifteen miles away in
the next county went in strong for baseball and foot racing and
turned out a team that could give a busy afternoon to towns two or
three times their size. Wherever they went, a crowd of rooters
went with them, not only to cheer but also to bet. Those were good
times for coal miners and pay was high by our standards. The
rooters were well supplied with folding money, and in the early
stages of the game the betters walked up and down in front of
improvised bleachers displaying their money and looking for customers. If there were local laws against public betting they never
ran inside the baseball field when the miners were playing.

When scores were close and hits were important, men with
money on the game pleadingly offered "A dollar for a hit!" and if

a hit was forthcoming the lucky batter gathered in a small harvest of silver dollars from the dust at his feet. These miner-sportsmen were way over our heads and we witnessed their performances in silent awe and admiration. Our financial operations were limited to occasional collections to buy new balls. Players furnished their own bats and gloves, although most of us played barehanded. Charlie Glass was our most admired catcher for his willingness to stand close behind the bat sans mitt, mask, shinguard, and protector. It was not our hardihood but our lack of money that fixed the limit of our equipment. League balls cost a dollar or more and a lost ball might throw us into bankruptcy. Barring such a catastrophe, a ball stayed in play as long as the stitching held.

Picnics were favorite summer affairs, requiring usually an anniversary or an institutional celebration for an excuse. Farmers were not likely to get up picnics for the mere joy of communing with Nature. We were in close touch with Nature twelve months in the year and knew her for what she was, a cold-blooded jade who could deal blessing or blight with equal indifference. The Fourth of July was always a good time for a picnic, giving opportunity for patriotic display and gastronomic indulgence at the same time.

There were Sunday School picnics, Old Settlers' meetings, country school picnics, and sometimes political picnics. The last were opportunities for local candidates to point with pride or view with alarm, and I remember a few fiery speakers who really hit the ball in local estimation. Most of them were dull and fumbling and seemed as relieved as were their hearers when the last line was reached.

A Democratic flag-raising in the old village of Henderson sticks in my memory as one of my more embarrassing moments. Henderson was a quiet little community that had never known the blight of prosperity. Founded more than forty years before I was born, it was permitted to remain much as it had been from the beginning. The center of it was a grass-grown square, a real village green, with old houses, a church, and a few shabby store buildings ranged around it. The flagpole that was to bear the stars

and stripes was raised by manpower, operating pulleys. It had been duly set and the new flag float There was a barbecue with a fat steer playing the le of course there were speeches. There always were, opportunity.

Filled with food and weary of oratory, mindful I was in funds—one thin dime to be exact—I wand grocery store and nonchalantly spent my hoard for a hard candy, all-day suckers. As I paused at the doo where to go and what to do, a man touched me on jerked his thumb over his shoulder toward the store says you didn't pay him," he remarked loudly. Blushin I dragged my leaden feet across the store, now grown size, and dumbly handed over my dime. I'm sure the meant to smile indulgently, but to me it was a smirk and a lurking threat. I was young and self-conscious been caught in the act. That ended the day for me. begun happily and with high anticipation was ending and shame. For once I was glad to find myself on the Of such stuff are the tragedies of youth.

A social event of considerable magnitude was the c usually in early September. That was the week when catastrophe, however much it might be needed. The combination livestock show and exhibition of farm mach farm products, fruit, vegetables, grain, jams, jellies, pickles, rows of canned fruits from farm kitchens. Blue, white ribbons, emblems of awards, were proudly disp exultant winners. There were side shows too, the fat, or bearded lady, a snake charmer with a sluggish serpen around her, the Streets of Cairo with the barker making allusion to the daring dances performed inside, the grisl unearthed in a cellar somewhere, record of a mysterious In the afternoon there were running and trotting races, benefit of pari-mutuel.

One popular feature was the balloon ascension. This drew a crowd, from the building of the fire that heated

One game, name forgotten, called for the putting of a man's
hat on a girl's head to this refrain:

So take this hat on your head,
Keep your head warm,
And take a sweet kiss,
It will do you no harm ,

suiting the action to the words. To see my favorite schoolteacher
of the moment meekly accept this salute from a young man whom
I held in particular dislike was almost more than I could bear.

The reason for widespread objection to dancing and bland
approval of kissing games closely resembling a country dance is
for social psychologists to think about. We did not bar the fiddle
as a musical instrument because of its association with the dance.
Win Terpening, with an endless repertoire of old dances for his
fiddle, was in demand as a complete entertainment in himself.
I heard them all, "Money Musk," "Irish Washerwoman," "Arkan-
saw Traveler," "Buffalo Gals, Are You Comin' Out Tonight?"
"Oh, Susannah," and many more, over and over, times beyond
memory, and I never heard Win criticized for playing or myself
reproved for listening.

The sin of dancing was not in the fiddle. I have heard country
people call waltzing "hugging to music." But we enjoyed music,
at least our kind, and I know of no Illinois Blue Law against hugging, with or without music. The American frontier danced all
the way from Virginia to Oregon, but it did not waltz. Perhaps
it was the waltz that introduced sin. When I first saw waltzing
it seemed to me a dull and spiritless way of wasting time, not to be
compared with rabbit hunting or lying on one's back in the shade
and dreaming. If waltzing was a sin, then sin was not as interesting
as had been represented. It was all very bewildering.

Win and his fiddle should not be dismissed lightly. He was
of the old breed. Tucking his instrument against his shoulder, not
his cheek, with one leg crossed over the other, beating time with a
foot on the floor, he launched into melody. As the music maker
played, the small boy saw visions and dreamed dreams. Men rode
hard through the night on dangerous errands, legions marched out

of the mist, bands played, and crowds cheered. I have heard Ysaye and Kreisler and Menuhin, and lesser virtuosos, great musicians crowned with laurel and strung with decorations, but none of them had the power to send me wandering as had Win. Pleasant dreams to him wherever he sleeps!

There were other makers of music among us, Ed Allen with his banjo, for example. His favorite selection was "The Son of a Gamboleer." The unco guid of the community viewed this one with some doubt. "Gamboleer" was probably vernacular for "Gambler" and so was perhaps barely admissible, but two of the lines were clearly attaint "Like every honest fellow I drink my lager beer / Like every honest fellow I take my whiskey clear / I'm a rambling rake of poverty / The son of a gamboleer." Was this a good example to set before innocent and impressionable youth? One youth at least listened with pleasure but without perceptible desire to imitate.

We had many harmonica players; we called it "mouth organ." This could deliver stirring music, especially in the moonlight with the shadows of leaves lying on the grass and crickets chirping. In the hands of a master the harmonica could be plaintive and wistful too. Dan wasn't addicted to music, but he occasionally ventured to perform on an instrument known as a "jew's-harp." The result was only remotely musical.

If there was a cottage organ in the house, a gathering of youth was likely to develop into a songfest, with Stephen Foster of course, "My Old Kentucky Home," "Way Down Upon the Suwanee River," "Old Black Joe," and the like, and current favorites, "Only a Bird in a Gilded Cage," "Two Little Girls in Blue." If the singers really developed a full head of steam, there was certain to be a hymn or two, just to remind us that man was mortal.

We read little and our knowledge of literature was slight, but that did not deter us from organizing Literary and Debating societies. That was the twilight of the old Lyceum, and if it hadn't been, we were beneath the notice—and price—of the famous figures of the platform. As with so many things, if we wanted intellectual entertainment we must provide it ourselves. So we debated. Some

of the questions that come down to me are alluring with their naive
hints of philosophic entanglement. "Resolved, That the pen is
mightier than the sword," was one. Another was, "Resolved,
That the love of money is the root of all evil." I have a dim impression that I took part in the latter, but I have no recollection whether
I was for money or against it. Prohibition was a favorite theme,
the judges invariably finding against the demon rum, whatever the
merits of the argument. Nevertheless, the saloon business in nearby
Galesburg and Monmouth continued profitable.

We seemed never to debate contemporary problems, tariff,
civil service reform, the waste of public lands, railroad rates, and
dwinding farm incomes. These were all important issues, but we
expressed no views and reached no decision, indicating that we
had not become politically awake and articulate in national affairs.
The stormy decade of the nineties was still to come.

Our opportunities to sit at the feet of oratorical greatness were
limited, but our appreciation of the power of the spoken word was
real. No Websters or Lincolns came our way, but thin and
shadowy as the local equivalents were, we listened and admired. A
candidate for Congress was by right and of necessity an orator and
a candidate for the state legislature was assumed to be worth hearing, whatever his politics. If a candidate was weak on evidence
and argument, there was always the fall of Rome and the greatness
of America to fall back on. English tyranny was always a sound
play, to the great annoyance of Father and Uncle Jim.

Campaign speeches were infrequent and only mildly entertaining, but our social life we had with us always. A favorite
pastime on summer evenings was the Ice Cream Sociable, highly
regarded as a means of making money for church or Sunday School
or similar worthy causes. Most of the real fun was in the preparation. Japanese lanterns were strung from trees and posts, tables
were improvised with rough boards, tickets were printed by hand,
and there remained only to provide the ice cream and cake that
were the standard fare. If there had been a good strawberry season
an extra ten cents could be tacked on the usual charge of a quarter.

Usually some farmer not too far away had an icehouse filled

with cakes cut from an artificial pond and stored against the coming heat. We made the ice cream ourselves, spelling each other in the long turning of the freezer, also borrowed from the owner of the icehouse. As night approached the weather became the burning question. If clouds gathered in the southwest, heralding a thunderstorm, spirits sank as the afternoon wore away. Would the wind shift and give the rain to someone in less need of clear skies and dry grass? Our prayers were not always effective, but rain or no rain, the sociable was held at the appointed time. Even small houses had possibilities on such nights.

The real crisis came with the counting of the receipts. Our scale of operations and also our estimate of possible profit was modest. Because most of our expense was our own labor and time, we usually came out with a perceptible balance. And if there was a deficit, what of it? Win or lose, we had had a good time.

Small boys who lived not too far from each other occasionally exchanged visits, sometimes overnight. Three, sometimes four, in a bed was not too many. Kicking each other out of bed was good fun, but it had its hazards if it became too noisy. Leavetaking at the end of a daytime visit had its own variation with us, different from the lingering farewell at the door of the older ones. With boys the protocol required the host of the moment to walk part of the homeward way with the visitor. This was "going piece ways." For the host to decline would have been a serious affront.

It has become a fixed belief in America that the old-fashioned farmer was the perfect individualist. Maybe so, but he was also gregarious. Even a funeral gave opportunity for neighborly chat, in a reverently subdued tone of course. Every crossroads store was a social center and the most casual meeting an occasion for the exchange of local news. The farmer who lived the life of a hermit usually had something wrong with him.

CHAPTER XIV

How Did We Talk?

T HE NUMBERS of people, men and women, old and young, involved in our westward movement can only be estimated roughly by noting the rate of growth of the Western States. The figures for California are eloquent, slightly over ninety thousand in 1850, today crowding twenty million, mostly native born but not in California. Our immigration statistics are more illuminating; beginning with 1820 approximately forty-two million from overseas have been added to our total count. Naturally in such a tremendous shifting of human beings many things were changed, our dress, our occupations, our speech. In general, we thought of ourselves as English somewhere back, but what does that mean? The speech of Sussex is not the speech of Northumberland and the accent of the London Cockney differs from both. In our small countryside could be heard traces of the broad A of Massachusetts and the soft drawl of Virginia. The process of change continued to work as we moved westward with new experiences and associations adding new elements to the conglomerate of our speech to change us still further. Some of the elements so added had historical backgrounds of their own. Jerry Hawkins had come among us from somewhere in eastern Kentucky, our only hillbilly. When Jerry said: "Do you want me to *hope* you with your threshin'?" we thought of it as only another of Jerry's many oddities. Much later when I explored the *Canterbury Tales* in college I learned that the unlettered hillbilly was speaking an

155

English older than Shakespeare, Chaucer, and beyond: "That hem hath *holpen* whan that thy were siecke." Jerry was old-English.

Another contribution was "Friday week" as a definite date, meaning a week from Friday. This at first confused then annoyed me. Why not say what he meant and be done wih it? For all my annoyance Jerry continued his confusing habit until the day he died, and he lived to be over ninety.

For most of us the words of greeting were obvious and commonplace, "Good morning," "How do you do?" "How are you?" frequently contracted to "Har you?"—but not with "Uncle" Robert Adcock with Virginia in his near background. With him the word was "Howdy," and when he spoke it to a small boy the effect was curiously that of a benediction endowing the boy with an individuality not often conceded by his elders. Somewhere along the way I encountered the phrase "What's the good word?" I never knew the proper response to that one. A few Missourians had drifted upriver to us, bringing a locution that puzzled me for a long time. For most of us evening was the time between supper and bedtime, but evidently in Missouri evening began right after midday dinner; there was no afternoon, even for lotus eaters.

With the Britts there were a few words that I recall as peculiar to us, part of the scanty luggage that they brought with them from the Old Country. Most of these Father had set himself to discard as part of the process of naturalization, mere vestiges of an England that he had put behind him, although for him "were" and "been" were as they had been in England, not "wur" and "bin." Uncle Jim, his older brother and the first comer to America, was loath to lay the old aside. As has been said, February was "Febivary" as long as he lived and put was "putt," as in golf. Both families spoke of a "wamus," sometimes "wampus," meaning a light denim work jacket. Did it mean "warm us?" Perhaps. It was Uncle Jim who made for his two sons a crossbow that was a fair reproduction of the weapon that both Normans and Saxons had used in the Battle of Hastings. That was an appropriate survival, for the place where the battle was fought was in the home country that Bretts and Fosters knew, and as boys both brothers had played over the ruins of the old Abbey marking the spot where King Harold died. For both the term for England was most often the Old Country. To look ill or depressed was to look "old-fashioned," in Father's vocabulary.

Mother used aphorisms that hinted at the past. "Waste not, want not" was one of these and it was applied rigorously in the household operations. Akin to this was a warning often leveled at me when I was caught taking more than I needed of some article on the table, sugar probably. That was a sign that a day would come when I would go hungry for that particular thing. Of a young man who had married a girl with what Mother regarded as toplofty social ambitions, she foretold drily: "He'll come to hard work before he dies." And he did. Of course we used phrases that were native products. Many years later I asked a brother about a man we had both known as a boy in country school. "Is he working?" I inquired idly. My brother's answer was in eloquent vernacular: "He don't aim to!" There was no need of further light.

Such phrases as "Hit the nail on the head," "Hew to the line" were redolent of pioneer beginnings, as was "Calling a spade a spade." "Set your sights" required no translation to anyone familiar with the function of the rear sight of the old long-barreled rifle. "Take care of the pennies and the pounds will take care of themselves" was obvious wisdom in an economy that sent more pennies than pounds our way. "Hoe out your row" came from a primitive past before the horse-drawn cultivator had supplanted the humble hoe, but the variant "Hoe your own row" was an oblique way of suggesting that the other fellow mind his own business. "Tend to your knitting" was a progenitor of the modern "keep your eye on the ball." "Early to bed and early to rise makes a man healthy, wealthy, and wise" was misplaced in a time when all men went to bed early and got up with the sun or earlier. In that pre-electric time, darkness was the time for sleeping, but only a favored few achieved wealth or wisdom.

Court ship and marriage had their techniques and ceremonials of course, but I recall no talk of engagement and I was grown and in college before I heard anyone speak of his "fiancee" as of an obvious relationship. "Going together" was the proper term with us and the equity thus established was generally recognized by rival swains. Today's teenagers call it "going steady." Of the boy who betrayed his state of mind by an air of helpless enslavement it might be said that he was "sitting up to her like a sick kitten to a hot brick."

Weddings were generally held in the bride's home; at least I recall no church ceremonies. Neither do I recall wedding "breakfasts," although the word "infare" comes to me vaguely, defined by Webster as wedding reception or "housewarming." The first night after the ceremony was usually spent at the bride's home and the second at the groom's. Then the happy couple settled in their new home, wherever it might be. Honeymoons shone only in romantic novels.

A feature of a wedding was a "shivaree" that usually took place the first evening. (I was a proud boy when I found the proper spelling was "charivari.") However it was spelled or pronounced, the institution remained the same, a discordant concert of horns, tin pans, shotguns fired in the air, horse fiddles, anything to make a noise. It was usually mercifully brief, then the door opened and the makers of noise trooped into the house to be treated to cigars by the provident groom. My dictionary states solemnly that this celebration was aimed only at an unpopular pair and was intended as an insult. It was not so with us.

The cryptic slang of the day filtered through to us in due course, and we said "Skiddoo!" "Twenty-three," and "You know it" as glibly and with as little sense as did the town boys. There were other phrases that were closer to the grass roots. The sound of distant thunder was "the devil's potato wagon crossing a bridge," and "like a bat out of hell" connoted great speed. "Like hell abeatin' tanbark" also suggested speed or vigor. "Taking a fall out of him" was not a wrestling term but a serious affair with bare knuckles. When two boys on the playground stood toe to toe to test which would first back away, they were "chugging," not boxing, and a similar test with hazel switches instead of fists was "lick jacket."

"Mad as a wet hen" was the ultimate in anger. Those who have seen a wet hen will understand.

When a man was suspected of a feeling of superiority, he thought he was "a somebody." Undue individualism was to be "independent as a hog on ice." For some reason, beans entered rather largely into our common speech. One who "didn't know beans" was plain stupid, and one who knew "how many beans make five" was smart beyond the average. Poor soil "wouldn't grow white beans."

We had no colored families in our neighborhood, so there was no hint of an Uncle Remus influence in our talk or our ideas, but we picked up bits of Swedish words and phrases, some of them probably improper. Some words of common use were beginning to have a tinge of vulgarity. Such a one was "puke." To us all Missourians were pukes as all Illinoisans were suckers. Why? Don't ask me. The people of Iowa were Hawkeyes, of Indiana, Hoosiers, of Ohio, Buckeyes. Today an old-time Oklahoman is a Sooner, reminiscent of the opening of the Cherokee Strip in 1893.

By the time I was a senior in college, I regarded myself as a purist in speech, only to be called sharply to account by my favorite professor John P. Cushing for saying "I didn't get to go" when he asked me if I had heard a certain visiting lecturer. "Young man," he said, "if you intend to live in New York or anywhere in the East 'get to go' will mark you as a provincial." But I wondered; to me it suggested a definite interference with my plan to attend. John P. found our Illinois speech sometimes quaint, as when a student said of his sheepskin coat "It turns the wind." Another Easterner was vastly amused by our common statement "The dog wants out"—or in. We said "down cellar" because that was where the cellar was, but we didn't say "Up attic" as New Englanders do—probably because we had no attics. Participles bothered us, especially when we were trying to speak correctly, when something like this might emerge "I seen him yesterday but I ain't saw him today."

Then as now college faculties were much concerned over the shortcomings of freshmen in the writing of their mother tongue, their limited vocabularies, their spelling, their use of punctuation marks, all the standard complaints. Then as now there was a wide variation in the cures prescribed by faculty experts, only an occasional eccentric member venturing to suggest that the way to learn how to write was by writing until it became as natural a means of communication as speaking. It must be remembered that writing is an acquired art that many never learn.

The procedure that I encountered at Knox in the middle nineties was the writing of short daily themes by all freshmen on whatever subjects the victims could dig up in their desperation. The grading of these daily agonies was one of the minor duties of Billy Simonds, who was wont to let off steam by reading some of the more amusingly atrocious specimens when it became his turn in the daily chapel talk. One that is recalled dealt with the railroad trip from home to college to endure the freshman initiation. The final phrase was the payoff line: "Then I closed my eyes and became obvious to my surroundings." (The writer may have been right at that.)

It was my good fortune to enjoy putting words on paper. I had been scribbling ever since I learned to push a pen to some vague purpose, and the choice of a subject for my daily theme was seldom difficult. It might be a For Sale sign on an old house, the legends on a freight car rumbling over a railroad crossing on the way to college, the pouring of molten iron in a foundry glimpsed through an open door. Of course, as is the manner of most beginners in this strange art, my early efforts were largely imitative, perhaps the style of an adventure story by J. T. Trowbridge in the *Youth's Companion*. Many times I did my best to construct a yarn in the Trowbridge manner out of the everyday people and things of our farm. They were pretty feeble and were seldom finished, but unconsciously I was learning to write a long time before I set foot on a college campus.

Closely allied with our manner of speech were bits of folklore that were accepted by us as gospel truth: You can kill a snake, but its tail will not die until sundown. If a snapping turtle lays hold of you he will not let go until it thunders. I never saw that tested.

A sure cure for a side that ached from too much running was to turn over a dry clod, or better still a small flat stone if you could find one, spit under it and replace it. Care must be taken not to look back as you walked away. (Too bad Lot's wife didn't know that.) Warts were caused by touching toads. The howling of a dog at night meant that death was near. All dogs howled on moonlight nights and therefore death was always somewhere about. When one of us sneezed, it was proper procedure to exclaim: "God bless you!" There was reason behind this age-old practice. A symptom of one of the medieval plagues was violent sneezing. Opening an umbrella in the house brought bad luck and so did watching a departing guest out of sight. Another bringer of ill fortune was to walk under a ladder, possibly a reminder of the day when gallows graced the roadsides of England.

With our folklore as with our speech, we were the residuary heirs of a long line of cultures, habits, experiences, and fears. Shadowy figures centuries dead walked with us along our Illinois roads.

※※

Chapter XV

The Boy Goes To College

IN MY seventeenth year a long-cherished dream began to take tangible form. I won the family consent to "go away to school," with college as the ultimate goal. When I made serious proposal of this radical step, Father offered a mild alternative of a course in the state agricultural school at Urbana. It was unthinkable to him that his youngest son was not content to be a farmer as he had been and he wanted to be sure that I should be a good one. This did not fit into my plan of some sort of a professional career as far as possible removed from the drudgery of farming. My stubborn insistence on college prevailed, but it was still viewed as a rash idea, just the sort that I would entertain. We had no family tradition of college and no one of our kin had ever been adorned with a degree.

The nearest approach to it was my cousin Joe, son of my Uncle Jim, who had had two terms in the Knox Academy and had impressed his teachers with his dogged drive and his intelligent persistence. Then he turned to teaching country school, married another country teacher, and went homesteading in Nebraska. It is worth noting that all of their six children graduated from college. That was the sort of thing that happened many times in our America.

That I should even have thought of such a step as college is to be written down to the credit of the wide-open immigration laws of that time. Had I been born in England, the son of a workingman, or even a small tenant farmer, the hope of any education be-

163

yond the most elementary level would have been a fantastic dream. Thomas Hardy made *Jude the Obscure*, dreaming of Oxford, a figure of tragedy. It was not so in America. For more than two centuries this country really was the haven of the oppressed. Now its doors are opened to only a favored few, not a cause for national pride.

"Going away to school" sounded impressive, smacking of ivy-covered towers and quiet cloisters. In reality my transmigration was only twelve miles in distance, though much further in significance. Knox College was in Galesburg; historically speaking it *was* Galesburg. In 1835 a company of high-minded, land-hungry souls in and around the little town of Whitesboro, New York, near Utica, had agreed to find an attractive location somewhere in the West and there to found a college, a church, and a community free from the corrupting influences of the crowded East. The site they selected was midway between the Illinois and Mississippi rivers, on the imperceptible height of land that divided the waters between the two streams.

It was not a haphazard choice. A committee had been sent a year before to spy out the land. The soil was fertile and well drained, and land was to be the basic capital of the new enterprise. A large tract, nearly eighteen thousand acres, was bought by the colony at the government price of $1.25 an acre and resold to individual members for a minimum of $5.00 an acre. The profit was for the building and endowing of the college, ultimately nearly $40,000, a large sum for that day. Families buying as much as eighty acres from the common holding received a scholarship right covering tuition fees in the new college for twenty-five years of actual use. Nearly a hundred years later there was still a student or two benefiting from this original foundation. The scholarship land plan was so successful that it came near wrecking the college before it was fairly launched. It has been estimated that before the college doors opened, the infant institution was in debt for two thousand and fifty years of free tuition.

There was another reason for the selection of a site far away from the two rivers that were highways for early settlers. Rivers brought trade, but trading centers were also centers of sin. So the founders of the new college sought the free and sinless air of the open prairie. Less than twenty years later, college and town worked mightily to bring the first railway through their midst, ignoring the fact that sin travels by rail as well as by water.

The college donated the land for the right of way through the town and the necessary station, but overlooked the fact that trains run on Sundays as well as weekdays. When realization of this sacrilegious practice came, the president of the college took his stand in front of the locomotive and forbade it to proceed. Said the engineer, "Get the hell out of the way or you'll be run over." Stubborn as he was, the president conceded defeat and the train went on its sinful way.

Knox was not the only college available in the early nineties. Between 1830 and 1860 colleges were sown thickly throughout Illinois, and by my time there were at least five others within a radius of fifty miles, all of them apparently hungry for students. One of them, Hedding, a Methodist outpost in Abingdon twenty miles away, sent a representative to see us. His argument was simple: "Send your boy to your church school. He'll be safe there." Father's Methodism wasn't that deeply rooted and he listened in silence. Knox never glanced in my direction, rather a blow to my ego. The mortality of those early colleges was high and four of these are no longer among the living, but narrow and poverty-stricken as they were, these struggling little colleges did much to relieve the cultural barrenness of the raw, new country. My mind was set on Knox and Knox it was.

The shift from the simplicities of farm living to the urban civilization of Galesburg, population about fifteen thousand, seemed bewildering to me. In reality it was merely a change from one aspect of early midwestern America to another. College, town, and farm were different phases of the same time and place, characteristic products of identical forces. I had known Galesburg from the time of my earliest memories as the place where we did most of our marketing. It was there that I had seen my first telephone and my first electric light and was to see my first trolley car. Now it was to be my home for nine months of the year.

Urban and urbane as the new environment seemed, the principal transition was from living at home in the country among familiar faces to living in a furnished room in town surrounded by strangers, and from the smell of wood smoke to the reek of soft coal. We country folk had viewed townspeople with an unfriendly and suspicious eye. Now I was to live among them and in time to be one of them.

The college took no responsibility for the housing of men students, leaving them to shift for themselves around the town. I was already provided with a roommate, the son of another farmer in the Tylerville neighborhood who was setting forth on the same exciting adventure, and we had such consolation as could be found in being fellow-exiles. Both of us were acutely homesick at intervals for much of the first year and neglected few opportunities for weekends at home. More than once when winter mud made country roads impassable we walked the ten long miles across the bleak, wind-swept prairie from Galesburg to Tylerville.

To the boy on the farm that road from home to "town" was more than a known number of slow miles. If he had known the right words he might have described it as a cultural adventure, a movement away from the familiar, simple, and primitive to the complex, sophisticated, and strange. He may have disliked the town boy, but he also envied him and tried to ape his easy assurance and his casual acceptance of things alien and sometimes terrifying. He traveled that road in dust, mud, snow, blistering heat and the freezing winds of winter. As he neared the miniature metropolis, signs on the fences teased him with the names of drygoods stores, jewelers, photograph galleries, even a bookstore, shoe stores, all waiting for him on Main Street and around the Square. Tattered posters on barns reminded him of the circus that had come and gone, and soon he could see the pall of smoke that hung over the railroad shops, the Brown Cornplanter Works, and Frost's Foundry. This was to be his world perhaps.

A diploma was seven years away. Founded in 1837, in common with most western colleges of that time, Knox had begun as an academy. The first class had graduated in 1846. The first duty of a new college was to prepare its students for admission. It is worth noting that of the twenty-one members of the first four graduating classes twelve became clergymen. The combination of prep school and college lasted for more than sixty years. The system had one advantage: if the candidate had passed his prep courses with satisfactory grades, he stepped into college with no formalities of aptitude tests or examinations. My IQ is unknown to me, even to this day. Because of this I am inclined to underestimate the machinery of superpsychological analysis that surrounds college admissions now. Undoubtedly they discover many things, but are they the important ones? Whatever the answer, the fifty of us who enrolled as Junior Preps on that September day knew only that we wanted to go to college.

Tuition charges were miscroscopic compared with modern demands, $45.00 a year in the college, $25.00 in the academy. Not until I was a senior did my expenses for the year, college and personal, exceed $200.00. Small as that seems now, it was not an insignificant sum in the nineties. Those were depression years for farmers. Farm prices were low, fifteen cents a bushel for corn, $3.75 per hundredweight for hogs, sometimes less. A dollar a day was the standard wage for ordinary labor, and a long day at that. A neighbor summed up the matter succinctly when he said. "It takes one man's wages to keep another man in school." Few of us, whether farm or city-bred, were from families that could view the cost of college with indifference.

The living problem of the new students was easily solved by renting a small furnished room at four dollars a month in a comfortable old house three blocks from the campus. Boarding houses were over our heads, five or six dollares a week for board and room. The college did have a college common of a sort. The girls' dormitory, originally known as the Knox Female Seminary—Sem for short—had a large, low-ceilinged dining room on the ground floor, which was open to men students at a weekly charge of three dollars. So, by parental advice, we signed up for the Sem. A fortnight of this feature of coeducation was all that I could stand. Neither of us had had the reputation of being shy with girls of our own age in country school, but these were college girls, unbelievably sophisticated, well dressed, and at ease. My appetite failed as I sat, tongue-tied and miserable, in their presence three times a day, and I fled from the Sem at the end of the second week. After a week or two of catch-as-catch-can eating in cheap restaurants on Main Street, a haven was found in an eating club, and eating clubs took care of me through most of my college years.

These were common solutions of the food problem in most small colleges of the region that lacked dining halls for men. A club was usually organized by an upper class student who undertook to find a convenient house with a moderately adequate cook and a not too incompetent waitress. The organizer ate free by virtue of his services as steward and general manager and the rest paid an approximate ten dollars a month. Allowance was made for absence three meals in succession and, with an occasional rebate for savings in costs, actual charges worked out at about two dollars a week. The food was plain, but there was plenty of it, our appetites were good, and the rough and ready fellowship and youthful repartee that enlivened the meals was a blessed relief from the formality of the girls' dining hall.

Many, particularly of the men students worked their way wholly or in part. Some of the families in town had need for a student to mow the lawn, saw wood, shovel snow, take care of a horse and cow and do the odd jobs generally for room and board. All of us worked in the summer to earn a few dollars against the next year's expenses.

A favorite summer job was selling books from door to door. The neophyte was given a preparatory training, usually by an older student who had made good in previous summers. Two basic rules are recalled: a) never let the prospect shut the door in your face—if necessary keep one foot on the threshold; b) talk so fast that the victim has no chance to say "No." It was work that called for a glib tongue and an impressive amount of brass. Not all of us could do it, but the life had its points for even a poor salesman.

Small towns were the best territory, and word soon got around the younger set that there were a couple of college boys in town, insuring much social activity. It helped a lot if one of them was a fair baseball player. Otherwise the local boys might resent this unfair competition.

Registration and residence requirements for preps were informal and largely at the pleasure of the principal of the Academy, who permitted me to do the spring terms of my first two prep years in absentia. Phil had bought a small farm near the home place and was running both establishments. As his hired man I drew down a wage of twelve dollars a month, clear profit in my pocket against the bills of the coming year. I would like to remember that I worked with a textbook strapped to my plow handles and spent my evenings over my Greek and Latin, algebra and plane geometry, but I didn't. Long days in the field made evening study profitless, although I managed a few hours on rainy days and Sundays. When school opened in the fall I volunteered no report, and the authorities asked no questions. At this distance my memory of the pages of Caesar's *Commentaries* that I failed to read is no dimmer than of those over which I spent many weary and wasted hours. Caesar was not one of my favorite writers.

When I entered in 1891 the curriculum still clung closely to the old model, little changed in fifty years: three years of Latin and two of Greek in preparation for the classical course, two years of both in college. The scientific course, leading to a B.S., required no Greek. Something called the literary course, specially favored by girls preparing to teach, laid more stress on modern language and earned a Litt. B. Since only one year of preparation was required for this course, we sterner souls viewed it with superior scorn as an easy road to a diploma. There were no electives for preps and none in college until the junior year. This was offset by the lack of any limitation on the number of hours carried in college, permitting the eager beaver to take on as much of an overload as his own endurance allowed, at his own risk of course. I learned later that in spite of my interest in extracurricular affairs I had earned the equivalent of a hundred and forty units, almost enough to entitle me to a Master's degree on top of the A.B. The record shows that my schedule was a curiously spotted affair, including, for no reason whatever, a course in Mechanical Drawing, a subject for which I was considerably unsuited, but I did learn how to draw a parabola with the aid of a couple of pins and a piece of string. Eliot had installed his system of free electives at Harvard, but Harvard was far away and the small western colleges stuck close to old patterns and known ways.

The classical course, with its emphasis on Latin and Greek, was in the old tradition, although the faith in it was beginning to weaken. The influence of public high schools and state universities was growing with their emphasis on the "practical" and the vocational. When I stepped on the Knox campus for the first time, neither college nor academy had made more than a faint beginning in the multitudinous group of social studies that now fill such a large space in college catalogues. There had been mild experiment with a course in political economy taught by the dignified and venerable old president, who leaned heavily on Francis A. Walker's pioneer textbook in that subject, an elementary outline of the *laissez faire* theories expounded by Adam Smith more than a hundred years before. The influx of teachers trained in Germany was being felt in eastern institutions, but few of our professors had had more than a year or two of advanced training anywhere.

In the sciences, chemistry and physiology, with a touch of geology, held the field. There was a small observatory with a correspondingly small telescope so there was work in astronomy, but no physics or biology. The college boasted a library of seven thousand volumes, official count, consisting chiefly of collections fathered by the two men's literary societies, the standard English classics, bound volumes of magazines, a few safe French and German masterpieces, and theological works and collections of sermons presented by loyal alumni. College libraries are favorite meeting places for boys and girls between classes and though ours was only a single room it too served that useful purpose. There could be worse functions.

The shortcomings of the library were not so much of a disad-

vantage as would be the case now. Courses stuck close to textbooks, which were supposed to contain the answers to all legitimate
questions. There was one course which had the imposing title of
"Mental and Moral Philosophy," the textbook a slightly modernized version of Paley's *Evidences of Christianity*. To my surprise
this was one of the books that I already knew, a timeworn copy of
it having been picked up by Father somewhere. In this course a
skeptical student who raised a question that fell outside the limits
of the textbook was rebuked by the venerable professor for assum-
ing that the book did not contain all that any right-minded student
should seek to know. Upper classmen preparing for debates or
oratorical contests, which were numerous, were supposed to draw
their material from their own inner consciousness. There was little
or no original source material available, so modern methods of
teaching were unknown.

This spartan regime threw a heavy burden on the teacher.
Students were forced to look to him, and to him alone, for their
intellectual nourishment. There was no barrage of assigned reading to shield the lazy or indifferent instructor. The real ones met
the challenge squarely and turned liabilities and limitations into
opportunities. Libraries and laboratories are not unmixed bless-
ings. Euclid's only equipment was a sharp stick and the sand at his
feet. An early teacher of physics at Knox told me that he was sure
he had done his best teaching when he was forced to improvise his
equipment as he needed it.

Curiously enough military drill was a required part of the
Knox curriculum for the men, a hangover from the stresses and
fears of Civil War time. In 1862 a congressman from Vermont,
Justin Morrill, introduced a bill for the setting aside of large tracts
of public lands for the establishment of state schools especially
adapted to the training of young men in agricultural and mechanical arts. That was the beginning of the state universities, now
such powerful factors in our educational program. Institutions so
created were to be required to provide instruction in the profes-
sion of arms. Other colleges were permitted to petition Congress
for inclusion in such a military plan. The trustees of Knox made

application and the Knox cadet corps was formed. Drill was compulsory for all freshman and sophomore men.

It was a far cry from the present R.O.T.C., but I suppose it had its points. The weapons were breechloading muskets of the Civil War vintage and the uniforms were gray, resembling those worn at West Point, paid for by the wearer. The drill was rudimentary, manual of arms, close-order formations, no summer camp drill, and no commission in the army reserve. To me it was stupid beyond words, and I was happy to get it behind me.

The first lesson that we new junior preps had to learn was that of shutting ourselves in our rooms and preparing for next day's ordeal in complete solitude, no easy task for boys and girls fresh from country schools where studying and reciting went on simultaneously in the same room. The doubtful consolations of radio were a long way in the future. My courses that year were first-year Latin, algebra, and physical geography, new subjects all of them. All classes met five times a week. It was my good fortune to have two inspiring teachers, Miss Ida McCall in Latin and George Churchill in algebra and physical geography. Miss McCall's name is in my list of great teachers. Handicapped by deafness though she was, she missed nothing, and inattention in her classes was a thing unknown. Even the dull pages of Comstock's *First Year Latin* came alive and acquired meaning in that narrow, dingy classroom.

Churchill was the principal of the academy as well as a full-time teacher and a figure of importance in the church and the town, organizer of the public library and in frequent demand as a surveyor. To see him come into his classroom in the morning, stepping lightly in spite of his bulk, black eyes sparkling under his stiff, iron-gray pompadour, was like hearing a bugle call. It was in his room that I made my first recitation in Knox Academy. Our names were not yet known to him, but that made no difference to Churchill. Turning away from the blackboard he shot a thick forefinger in my direction. "You boy on the end of the bench there," he said. I was to sit through many dull classes under uninspiring teachers before my years of prep school, college, and graduate school were behind me, but the omens of that first term were all favorable.

Another feature of the traditional regime that I encountered at Knox was compulsory chapel. Five times a week, from nine to nine-thirty, we were herded into the chapel to listen through devotional exercises, followed by a brief talk by some member of the faculty, occasionally relieved by the outpourings of a distinguished guest. Some of the guests were really distinguished. One who is recalled was Frederick Warde, a well-known actor of the time scheduled to appear that evening in a Shakespeare production at the local theater. Another was General John B. Gordon, a Confederate veteran who looked the part, gray frock coat, gray imperial, commanding presence, and a master of all the variations of southern oratory at its best. We were all expert judges of oratory and we gave the general a high ranking.

It did not take any of us long to discover that the teacher of chemistry, Albert Hurd, was a great person, a distinguished figure on this or any other faculty. Born in Canada of an old Tory family and trained at Middlebury College in Vermont, he had come out to Knox in 1850, planning to stay only long enough to become acquainted with the geology of that part of the Mississippi Valley and then go back to his beloved mountains of New England to spend the rest of his life there. The appropriate year of his return never came, and he died in Galesburg at the age of eighty, still teaching within a few months of his death.

To anyone who knew Knox while he was there the memory of Professor Hurd is inseparable from that of the college he served for more than fifty years. His stoop-shouldered figure, clad in a long black frock coat, usually stained with chemicals, a Gladstone collar with a black string tie, came and went from home to college as punctually as the bell that tolled our hours. His high-bridged nose gave him an antique Roman look, suggesting the faces on coins struck in the great days of the Empire. As a teacher he was severe but human, with a gift of humor often tinged with good-natured malice.

It was the tragedy of this old Roman to live long enough to

discover that the progress of scientific knowledge had outrun him and the textbook he had written, isolated as he was from the new books and the scientific journals. A new and stimulating young president found the means somewhere within the narrow budget of the college to send Professor Hurd to a meeting of the newly formed chemistry society in Chicago. The old man came back to the college sunk in black despair to announce that he had learned that he knew nothing about chemistry. That was the time he proved that his antique Roman look was not a counterfeit. He declared that he would teach no more chemistry and resisted all urging to the contrary. But he was not to end his teaching in such a summary fashion. There was need of a teacher of advanced Latin and the post was offered to Hurd. It was nearly half a century since the old man's college Latin and he had never taught it, but fifty years was nothing for a man who had taught himself to read French in the seventies of a busy life, and he turned his back on his laboratory and took up Latin with the enthusiasm of youth.

The fortunate students who sat in his class saw Latin taught as none of the rest of us had ever known it. For Hurd this was a living language, the embodiment of a great literature, and not a series of exercises in syntax; something to be read, not dissected. Where other students had toiled painfully through a page or two a day, parsing sentences, identifying conjugations and declensions, dealing with obscure idioms, Hurd's students found themselves reading ten or fifteen pages a day and liking it. When it suited his purpose, the teacher took over the reading, annotating and amplifying as he read, placing Quintilian, Tacitus, Lucretius, and the rest in the context of their time and relating them to our later day. It was teaching in the great tradition, far removed from the barrack yard drill that the rest of us had suffered. It was a black day for the classics when teachers began to justify their work on the ground of something called "mental discipline." Hurd knew that the discipline lay in the understanding of the thing read and not in the minor techniques of the reading.

As students few of us knew or cared much about such variations and shadings of character and ability among our teachers.

They were our task masters and some of them were tougher than others, dangerous characters, to be approached with caution and respect. Such a man was John P. Cushing who came to Knox fresh from a German university in my freshman year. His courses ranged widely over the whole field of social studies, history, economics, political institutions, education, money and banking, tariff history. College professors did little research and wrote few books in those dim days. Naturally not even a product of Leipsic could be expert in all these subjects, but he knew enough of all of them to let some light into our inner darkness.

Whatever his subject I took as much of Cushing as I could cram into my schedule, barring only history and Theory of Education and Pedagogy. Knox was on a three-term basis, each term approximately equal to two-thirds of a modern semester. As the curriculum grew, one-term courses appeared, making it possible for teachers and students alike to deal with a bewildering number and variety of subjects in four years, an impressive range of scholarly activity.

Cushing fascinated me, and not only as a teacher. His superb scorn of the fumbler, the bluffer, the chronically unprepared was wonderful to behold from a safe distance. More than once girls left his class in tears and without hope of comfort or apology from the man in the driver's seat. Some of the men hated him forever after, but those who endured him and learned to take his pace came away with a clearer understanding of the logic and pageantry of history. In his classes a grunt of approval was as good as a crown of laurel anywhere else.

Of course we who were students knew nothing of the finances of the college or of the faculty. By the standards of today, salaries of teachers were microscopic, and our allowances were in proportion. We were sure that the funds of the college were ample for its needs and we were concerned only with the contents of our own pockets. Years after I learned that the college books were balanced more than once by the sale of a farm or two, of which the college still owned several. Trustees must have known the inevitable outcome of this naive consuming of capital, but nothing seems to have been done. On one occasion an attempt was made to raise funds locally in aid of the college and the faculty joined with a generous grant of ten per cent of their pay for the year. As the top professorial salary was eighteen hundred dollars, that grant of ten per cent was more than generous, it was princely. The trustees showed their appreciation by allowing the cut to remain for a long time at the reduced level. That too I learned in later years.

In terms of the Middle West, Knox was an old college, one of the first settlers. The president and many of the faculty were old men, few of whom had done real graduate work. Only two sported the magic Ph.D., now so necessary. One of them had taken his degree at Strasburg and was to continue in the service of the college for more than forty years, much of the time its dean. This was Billy Simonds. His legacy to the college was a memory of unfailing kindness and courtesy, flavored with rich humor. His courtesy was unfailing, but those who tried to take advantage of it soon discovered a steel hand within the velvet glove. No student who knew him failed to do him honor.

I do not worship the Ph.D., and graduate study will not make a silk purse out of anything but silk. Most of these teachers were devoted to the college, but the work of the classroom was too often a dull business, for all that. There was little attempt to relieve the arid wastes of the textbooks on which we were forced to rely, except in the case of the heaven-sent geniuses who have been named. I took kindly to Latin and Greek and even won a prize in one or the other, but, alas, I cannot claim to have read the Horace, the Virgil, the Iliad, and the Crito that were on the list. As for Caesar, his account of the building of a bridge led me to conclude that assassination was about what he deserved. Through these and others we "parsed" our way, identifying idioms, fixing—or missing—the numbers of declensions and conjugations, spotting the ablative absolute and the passive periphrastic, endlessly repeating the routine of the elementary years. What could have been an adventure of the mind and the spirit became a matter of rote and routine.

Fortunately for us all, college is more than a series of courses,

requirements and credits. It is a place where the young live together for four years and in the course of them generate some ideas
and many activities. It is the later fashion to look back on the college of sixty years ago as a place of strict control and rigid discipline. That is not the way I remember it. Our contact with the
teachers was in the formal atmosphere of the classroom where
we sat in patient rows and tried to answer questions. The rest of
the time our teachers left us severely alone and we were equally
considerate of them. Whiting Hall did keep the girls within strict
boundaries of hours and conduct, at least in form. Late callers were
discouraged, and not in subtle ways, and lingering goodbyes on the
front steps were likely to be brought to an end by the appearance
of grim authority.

We of the other sex lived pretty much where and as we chose.
The college had a list of approved rooming houses, but no attempt
was made to limit us to these favored places or to regulate our
coming and going. When my timid soul led me forth from the
dining room of Whiting Hall, the good woman who presided there
made mild protest when I told her that I planned to buy a meal
ticket in a cheap restaurant on Main Street, twenty-one meals for
two dollars and a half, while I looked about. She feared that the
associations might not be of the best for the young and unformed.
Naturally I did not reveal the fact that the people who ate in Hawk-
inson's were the kind I had known all my life, shirtsleeved America,
and that I yearned to escape from the cultured quiet of the young
ladies' dining hall. Beyond this mild gesture there was no hint
of interest or disapproval on the part of the college. Where I ate,
or whether I ate, was entirely my own business.

This practice of ignoring our ways outside the classroom left
us free to develop such extra-curricular activities as we might
devise. Our athletics were entirely our own, unorganized, uncoach-
ed, and uncontrolled. Enrollment in academy or college met all
eligibility requirements and there was no limitation on the number
of years a man might play on whatever passed for the varsity team
of the moment. In consequence a good baseball player of mediocre
intellectual status or interest might appear in occasional classes in

the spring term of the academy, paying only formal tribute to the college rules of registration and attendance, but helping mightily on the diamond while the short season lasted.

It was of one such season that I was reminded fifteen years later. By that time I was a hardened New Yorker. A casual friend invited me to meet him for lunch, as friends usually do arriving late and bringing with him a stranger whom he introduced as "Don Marquis, the farmer poet." In the jumble of introductions my name was overlooked and I supplied it. "Not Albert Britt," the stranger exclaimed. I confessed my identity and inquired what he knew about Albert Britt. His reply was, "I played baseball with you in Walnut, Illinois, in the summer of '96 and I was crazy to go to college. You were a college man and you played a fair brand of cow pasture ball. I tried to make it two years later, but something went wrong with the work formula. I quit at Christmas time, but I can claim I went to Knox." That was the beginning of a long friendship with Don Marquis, to those who knew him the best newspaper columnist New York ever had.

Our football was not the highly organized and supervised game of today, with impressive coaching staffs, managers, ticket associations, press releases, and all the minutiae of great enterprise. Players bought their own equipment, with occasional collections to buy a new football. The team that possessed as many as three footballs in good repair in a single season was to be envied. The first coach to appear on the campus was there for only a few days before the final game, the "big" game of the schedule. He was brought to us by a small group of local alumni anxious to do their bit for higher education and whatever pay he received came from alumni pockets Officially the college ignored the whole business.

A change was coming and before I graduated there was new blood in the president's office and signs of a sense of faculty responsibility, to the annoyance of some of the older professors who were impatient of such child's play.

In spite of low costs and simple methods, athletic finances were in a state of chronic bankruptcy, the intensity of which varied with the good nature of the printers, sporting goods dealers, and other businessmen with whom we sought credit. Attendance at games was irregular and the lot of ticket sellers and gatekeepers was a vague one. Town boys oozed through the fence at a dozen spots and free riders were almost as numerous as cash customers. Little attempt was made to provide grandstands or any kind of seats, and as the tension mounted the crowd moved out on the field in spite of feeble attempts to check them at the sidelines. More than once a fleet-footed halfback found himself threading his way downfield through spectators instead of opponents.

It was of this period that George Fitch wrote in his stories of Old Siwash, and Knox is the original Siwash as a result. Fitch was in the class ahead of me, but we had much in common, particularly a willingness to waste time together reading the immortal works of Bill Nye, later to serve as a rough model for Fitch's whimsical humor. His characters had occasional faint resemblances to men we both knew, but plots and incidents came mostly out of his own vivid imagination. It is in the color and the implications that those of us who remember that simple time find cause for faint twinges of nostalgia.

Our simple athletic ways gave little warning of the present colossal structure of stadia, players, coaching staffs, alumni chills and fever, and small fortunes in the box office at the end of the afternoon. Our humble efforts at least did not force upon us the indignity of defending football as a character builder or a means of valuable publicity. We played football because we liked it, and that was the beginning and end of our athletic philosophy. There have been worse reasons.

While we saw the beginning of college athletics, we beheld the twilight of a long-cherished student activity, the literary societies. In American college history these were almost as old as the colleges themselves, and Knox had her share, two for men in the academy and two in the college, and one each for women. As in most colleges, the classical tradition prevailed in their christening, Adelphi, Gnothautii, Zetetici, E.O.D., the last being the abbreviation for *Einai ou dokai*, "To be, not to seem." Adelphi was the oldest, founded in 1846, the year that saw the first senior class graduate. All these names emphasized the importance of knowledge, Gnothautii, *Gnothi seauton*, "Know thyself," Zetetici, "Seek to know." If any classicist questions the accurary of translation, this witness answers only that that was what we were told. In naming the society for college women a concession was made to the intellectual limitations of the weaker sex, and L.M.I. stood for Ladies' Mutual Improvement Society, at least voicing a pious hope. The prep girls also broke the classical pattern with Oneota, usually explained as an Indian word, tribe unnamed, meaning "The pursuit of fine arts." The translation was official, otherwise unverified. It can be found in the catalogues of the period.

Most of us belonged to one society or another, although fraternities and sororities were making inroads and attendance at meetings was dwindling. The programs were of the orthodox variety, prayer by the society chaplain—a senior heading for the ministry or the mission field—essays, declamations, debates, occasionally something called an oration, with a tumultuous business meeting to close the evening. For those who really worked at it, these meetings gave excellent training in extempore speaking and in parliamentary proceedings as set forth in Roberts' "Rules of Order."

Adelphi and Gnothautti alternated in the sponsoring of a lecture and concert series for which tickets were sold to town and gown. Some of the features were headliners that were counted on to carry weaker numbers. One of these was Leland T. Powers, elocutionist," who gave dramatic recitals from such features as *Tale of Two Cities*, a sure winner; another was the violinist Camilla Urso. Miss Urso was a hunchback, almost a dwarf, with the long sad face of one acquainted with suffering, but with her violin she evoked melodies that even the more critical angels must have noted. This series had been a sound profit-maker for years, but in the nineties attendance began to languish and red ink appeared on the balance sheet, and in my senior year it was my melancholy duty to announce a deficit large enough to discourage further ventures. Only the topnotchers could fill the house and our town was not large enough to carry a series of big names. The society lecture programs were embalmed in history.

Oratory still flourished and this was a Knox specialty. Early in the seventies, two members of Adelphi, facing a crisis in society finances, evolved the idea of an oratorical contest in which many colleges would participate. The suggestion was snapped up by other colleges and soon an elaborate organization of local, state, and interstate contests appeared. Thus was another deathless campus tradition born, at least to live out the century of its birth, not a bad record for a deathless tradition. At its high point, ten states were included and the final contests drew crowds that professional performers might have envied. There are distinguished names in the list of winners. William J. Bryan took a second in the interstate while a student at Illinois College, and Albert J. Beveridge, later senator from Indiana and author of distinguished biographies of Chief Justice Marshall and of Lincoln, took a first for DePauw and the State of Indiana. Knox was not only the originator of the idea, but also took rather more than her fair share of honors. One of the early champions was Edgar A. Bancroft, Knox '78, later leader of the Chicago bar, dying as Ambassador to Japan. Another was John H. Finley, '87, whom I first knew as the young and stimulating president of the college. In the same roll of honor are Otto Harback, '95, later to acquire fame as a creator of musical comedies, and William Gorsuch of my class, who died far too early as a teacher of speech in Marcus Whitman College in the State of Washington. At its zenith, the star of oratory shone high and bright, but with the coming of the new century its brightness soon grew dim and disappeared. It was a good day while it lasted.

Harback had the good fortune to win the interstate crown in Galesburg, and as a freshman I sat in the crowded auditorium and thrilled at the spectacle. One of the judges of delivery was the young and handsome Bryan and as he walked down the center aisle I heard a whisper run along the seats, "There's Bryan!" His nomination for the Presidency was only a year away, and he was already known through the midwest as a master of the spoken word. He passed an arm's length away and his flamboyant presence is still clear to me: high-bridged nose, masterful bearing, long black hair carelessly tossed back from a high forehead, the Websterian look and manner, consciousness of power in step and pose. His ability to control the turbulence of a tired and angry convention was no surprise to those who had seen or heard him. I remember too the celebration that kept placid Galesburg awake through most of the night following the announcement of another Knox victory. Ours was an unsophisticated, inexperienced generation of course, but at least we knew the magic of the spoken word, a thing that electricity and celluloid could not match.

The successful orations were of an old model, of which Webster was the great example, more impressive to hear than to read. An epigrammatic sentence expressed the wisdom of a century or an era, and the future was revealed in a glittering galaxy of phrases, more notable for showiness than for accuracy. The opening sentence of an old prize winner is still recalled. The subject was "The Loneliness of Genius," a characteristically rhetorical title, and the first sentence read, "Insects swarm, the lion walks alone," ignoring the fact that not all insects swarm and lions do not always walk alone. Another on John Brown closed with a sweeping prophecy: "The time will come when the hills of Old Virginia will echo back the answer No!" The exact question that was to have such conclusive answer is forgotten, but Virginia hills are still mute on the virtues of John Brown.

Few of the orators remain, but it is quite possible that the attics of old houses in Galesburg still hold a few battered copies of old orations. To read one of these to a roomful of modern students would produce only boredom and derisive laughter, but we lighted bonfires in the street and cheered ourselves hoarse to celebrate a victory. Those were simple days.

CHAPTER XVI

Oratory And Tumult

CHARACTERIZATIONS of the nineties are many and various. Thomas Beer, for reasons which remain obscure and unconvincing, called it the Mauve Decade and wrote a book about it under that title. The book is interesting and worth the reading, but as a justification of Mauve it remains somewhere short of final. It was the time of the "Yellow Book" in England, and to the avant garde in both countries yellow might well have been the color note. To the people now in college that decade is merely a marginal note in the long roll of decades that make up our national history. People lived then, to be sure, but why bother to give it a name at all? For us who lived then and felt the vibrations of the time, it was a period of hardship and conflict.

There had been signs and portents in the seventies and eighties. Strikes were frequent and often bloody. In 1886 occurred the "Haymarket Riot" with a bomb thrown into a column of police marching to suppress disorder that had not taken place.[1] Four men were hanged and three went to prison for life because

[1]There is an important footnote to the record of this trial. John Peter Altgeld became governor in 1892 and after a careful study of the case pardoned the men whose sentences had been commuted to imprisonment for life. The storm of abuse that greeted this courageous act moved Vachel Lindsay to write his well-known poem "The Eagle That Is Forgotten":
Sleep softly . . eagle forgotten . . under the stone,
Time has its way with you there and the clay has its own,
Sleep on, O bravehearted, O wise man that kindled the flame.
To live in mankind is far more than to live in a name,
To live in mankind, far, far more . . . than to live in a name.

183

they wore the label Anarchist and had been on the platform when the bomb was thrown. Six years later came the Homestead steel strike with a bloody battle between steel workers and Pinkerton detectives who were in the pay of the steel company. In 1894 a strike in the Pullman works spread to the railroads and regular troops were sent to Chicago to break the strike. Those were disturbing years.

In Illinois, and through the agricultural West generally, strikes and labor unions were regarded as distant, dangerous, and alien things, but the farmers had troubles of their own. Discontent had been growing ever since the Civil War and we in college knew of the Farmers' Alliance and its demand for the recapture of the political influence that farmers had once enjoyed, and the redress of pressing farm grievances. The year I began my work in Knox Academy saw the organization of a new party, the Populist, and we began to hear increasing demands for Free Silver, destined to fill the air in the campaign of 1896. A black year for farmers and wage-earners alike was 1893, a year of panic and disaster. Factories drew their fires, some never to light them again, banks closed their doors, and breadlines formed in the industrial towns.

This was also the year of the Chicago World's Fair, to those who saw it the greatest of all the world's fairs. Fortune made me one of the visitors. My oldest brother Fred, somewhere in Colorado decided to have a look and generously offered to take me with him. That was high adventure, the first time I had seen a big city or a body of water larger than an artificial pond in our neighborhood. It was also the first of my long railroad trips; all that and the big fair to boot.

We had been hearing about the fair plans for a year or more, the replicas of the ships of Columbus, the Court of Honor, the lagoons with genuine Italian gondolas propelled by real Italian gondoliers, the Midway with the ferris wheel, the reproduction of Blarney Castle with its famous stone, the Eskimos with their furs and their dogs, looking very uncomfortable in the heat of an Illinois summer. My brother and I trudged miles every day in a determined effort to see everything. I'm sure we missed a few items, but not many, and the end of the long day found us not only hungry but weary beyond all telling.

Youthful memories are tricky things and so it happens that my proudest recollection is of the gargantuan dinner I ordered in the diner on the way back home. I was asked to choose from an over-crowded dinner list, price one dollar. I cannot pretend to recall individual choices, but even our colored waiter was impressed. For once a dining car kitchen owed me nothing, for huge as my order was I cleared my plate.

I had my moments of wondering if the added burden of my school expenses would break the backbone of family finances and was promptly advised that my business was with books and not with banks or income. Another year would see me safely through the Academy and a full-fledged freshman and my interest in college journalism and debating was growing. Writing had drawn me ever since I had learned to read and I had experiemented with crude stories and essays while I was still in country school. One gem that I recall was a feebly satirical essay on the seasons that I read with great effect at a school "exhibition." It has been told that I was hailed as a youthful prodigy in country debating circles and I missed few chances to take the floor in Zetetici meetings.

About the time I slid into college, war broke out over the control of the college monthly, the *Coup d'Etat*, so-called because it had been the outcome of another college war ten years earlier. For some time the Barbs, as the non-fraternity men were called, had been chafing over the throttle-hold that fraternities had on this publication, and finally a new paper, the *Knox Student*, was launched. This was to be a weekly and devoted to college news, unlike the monthly *Coup d'Etat* which was concerned with "literature." The battle was a merry one while it lasted, campus politics being of the rough and tumble variety, but after two years of competition literature gave up the ghost and the *Student* held the field without competition, although never without criticism, as I had reason to know. Here was my opportunity to become a journalist and I promptly tried for, and achieved, a place on the staff, finally becoming editor in my senior year.

This was probably my most momentous decision. Previously I had taken it for granted that I would be a lawyer, and one of my less offensive nicknames had been "Lawyer." Now I was to learn the habit-forming effects of printer's ink, a weakness that has never wholly disappeared. Also I was to feel the intoxication of seeing in print words that I had written only the day before and to know the painful exhilaration of struggling to enclose ideas and events in phrases that a critical public was to read. There can be no other experience quite like it.

As with athletics, literary societies, and our other extracurricular activities, publications were left severely to whatever fate they might suffer at the hands of student editors. We did our work without censorship or assistance, at least in advance of publication. As to what happened after, that too was our risk. We made contracts, sold subscriptions and advertising space, and paid our bills—we hoped. If a profit remained at the end of the year it was divided between the editor and the business manager; if there was a deficit, that too was divided.

College journalism had its humors as well as its troubles and triumphs. Many of the local advertisers bought space on a trade basis. The resultant trade bills were ours to use or sell as we would or could. In my senior year the business manager and I had our hair cut, our pictures taken, our clothes pressed, and our shirts washed as extra dividends during the year. Even an undertaker's ad was "traded out," not for the disposal of a belligerent reader, but by the rental of folding chairs to college organizations in occasional need of extra seating space. It is not surprising to note that the business manager who achieved this feat went on to become a highly successful businessman.

It was in 1893, the year of disaster, that three Knox graduates, Sam McClure, John Phillips, and Albert Bird Brady, all of the class of '82, announced the launching of a new magazine, to be called *McClure's*. This is the story of a boy and a college, not a history of a man and a magazine, but we at Knox soon began to hear of man and magazine.

McClure had played some part in the selection of the youthful

John Finley as our president. Only five years out of college himself, the young head was a figure of drama and romance to many
of us, the country bred and ignorant. We did not know it, but the
college was quietly falling asleep before he came. Old ideas and
ways persisted in a world of rapid change. It was as though Finley opened doors and windows in a room of stale air and let fresh
winds blow through. He dramatized for us an outside world of
which we knew little, and slowly we realized that he was also dra-
matizing the college to that world. With his coming we "heard the
sound of a going in the tops of the mulberry trees," a sense of
new faces and exciting things.

He brought to us as lecturers people who were helping to make
history in many ways: Jane Addams, who told of the work that was
being done at a strange institution called a Settlement House in
the midst of Chicago slums. Jacob Riis, the police reporter turned
reformer, who told us of the sordid lives of the "other half" on New
York's East Side; Fridtjof Nansen, who came and received a doctor's degree, seeming more embarrassed than pleased by the honor.
That degree was the occasion for a snooty remark by the New York
Dramatic Mirror. "Everybody knows Nansen," said the *Mirror*,
"but who the hell is Knox College?" Finley was telling them. Ian
Maclaren, (John Watson), author of the *Bonnie Brier Bush*, was
welcomed by the college band, which played him through the
streets to the Union Hotel, to his great amusement. Eugene Field,
once a riotous student at Knox, returned and recited his verses of
childhood; Bob Burdette gave us an evening of his drily humorous
recitations; and Anthony Hope read some of his "Dolly Dialogues,"
delighting and puzzling us with his rich English drawl.

That was the time when the chubby little genius, William
Rainey Harper, was spreading the fame of his new University of
Chicago through the land, and his University Extension lectures
brought us such men as Harry Judson in history and that queer
compound Frederick Starr, eccentric, dogmatic, and master of a
wealth of strange lore in anthropology and other things. Frederick
Turner of Wisconsin, discoverer of the influence of the frontier
in American history, lectured to us, as did Richard T. Ely, the

revolutionary economist under whom Finley had studied at Johns Hopkins.

New faces and subjects appeared among the faculty. Biology came in the person of "Jimmy" Needham, a Knox graduate trained at Johns Hopkins. With his coming, microscopes were indicated and two were unearthed about the campus. Unfortunately one of them lacked an eyepiece and the other was the property of another member of the faculty, who promptly reclaimed it. Laboratory work in biology was forced to wait for equipment, and the young biologist added solid geometry to his scientific duties in order to fill out his schedule. Such knowledge as I still retain of solid geometry is due entirely to Jimmy Needham and not to any special aptitude that I discovered in myself.

The college was changing rapidly and by the time I became a junior the curriculum had been so altered that I could almost claim to have transferred to another college.

It was one of the proud memories of Knox that it had played host to one of the Lincoln-Douglas debates, the fifth, but there had been no celebration of that event. The new president's instinct for the dramatic led him unerringly to Lincoln-Douglas, and the day of the debate, October 8, became a marked occasion. At the first ceremony we heard Chauncey M. Depew, Senator from New York and an orator of the old school. On that day a tablet set beside the entrance to Old Main to commemorate the debate was unveiled. That too was something new in the college program, deepening our sense of being a part of historical process and giving us at least a listening acquaintance with authentic greatness.

The tablet was to have a more than local significance. About that time a youngster, the son of a Swedish immigrant, was doing odd jobs around the town, delivering newspapers, running errands, mowing lawns, anything to help out the slender family income. His work took him across the campus, and he stopped to read the inscription with its quotation from Lincoln's speech and felt a stirring in his imagination. Lincoln had known poverty and obscurity and had climbed to enduring greatness. The lesson was plain and it was not to be forgotten. Thirty years later Carl Sandburg published *The Prairie Years*, the first volume of his monumental life of Lincoln. The immigrant's son had paid his debt to the New World.

A problem that the new president of Knox faced was the celebration of Washington's Birthday, one of the sacred traditions of the campus. In addition to the obvious observances with music, oratory, and drama, all in appropriate Revolutionary costume, the students had made it the occasion for battle between preps and college men. The mission of the preps was to make their way in the darkness of the night before to the belfry on Old Main that housed the college bell and there announce their triumphant presence by ringing the bell lustily. College students rushed to the attack and the battle raged on stairs and roof. The climax came in my freshman year when the hard-pressed preps armed themselves with bricks from the unused chimneys that dotted the roof of the old building, to the great embarrassment and considerable bruising of the college men. Don't ask how this cheerful pastime originated or why. Truly wonderful and past all knowing are the ways of youth in college.

Something had to be done and the resourceful president resurrected another anniversary. According to the record, the legislative charter that gave the college official being had been signed by the governor on February 15. This date had been ignored for sixty years as of no special significance, but it came providentially to the presidential mind. A holiday on February 15 might enable the college to soft-pedal the birthday of the first President only a week later. Strangely it worked and the Washington's Birthday riots passed into history.

As Sam McClure had played some part in the discovery of the new president, it was only right and proper that he should become a trustee, a frequent visitor, and an occasional chapel speaker. Later I knew him much better, but in those days he was a fabulous figure, a maker of magic. He was a genius, with all the unpredictability of that species to boot. Without capital and with limited experience, he and his two classmates and associates worked a revolution in magazine publishing. We had known the old-style magazines, the work of the older masters, *Harpers's, Century, Scribner's,* the *Atlantic,* the *North American Review,* the *Forum.* Of this galaxy only two remain to this later day. Their literary merit was beyond question, but their kind of literature left the younger generation cold. Their ideals were high, but the language they spoke was not ours. From the beginning, *McClure's* dealt with the world in which we lived. In its pages we found new names and new themes: Rudyard Kipling, with his exciting tales of the life of the English rulers of India, still to be read in *Plain Tales from the Hills, Soldiers Three, Stories of Mine Own People;* Stevenson, with *Treasure Island, Kidnapped* and *David Balfour.* Octave Thanet (Mary French) who hailed from Davenport, Iowa, almost next door to us, with pictures of the lives of the kind of people we knew.

Ten cents was the key that unlocked the door to such fresh experiences as Anthony Hope's *Prisoner of Zenda* and young Booth Tarkington's *Monsieur Beaucaire,* followed by *The Gentleman from Indiana.* If this was literature, and much of it was, it was a new kind to us and more real and compelling than the work of the great Brahmins who had ruled us from their cultural heights in Boston and Cambridge, and we began to read for the sheer pleasure of vicarious experience. If any inquiring reporter had polled the students of the late nineties to discover what they read, the names we have mentioned would have been high on every list. The glory of *McClure's* lasted only a few years, but before it passed from the scene the revolution it launched had been accomplished, to the great benefit of magazine readers.

We had one intellectual treat that is denied to most college students today, the chance to see plays professionally, and sometimes competently, produced. Road companies were still in their glory and most of them came to our town sooner or later. We saw most of the stars of the stage: Otis Skinner, Richard Mansfield, Frederick Warde, the younger Sothern, Francis Wilson, and many lesser lights. There was Walker Whiteside, the Edwin Booth of the road in the nineties. He gave us "Hamlet," "Ruy Blas," "Richelieu," "Romeo and Juliet." Our theatrical bill of fare was a mixed one. I sat in the top gallery to see the new heavyweight champion James J. Corbett do his stuff as "Gentleman Jim," and I can testify at least to the dramatic quality of his bag-punching act. A memorable evening was Hamlet played by an Italian, Alessandro Salvini, son of the great Tomaso. The climax of the performance was the ghost scene, where Salvini tore passion to shreds, stamping across the stage, waving his sword wildly, shouting his outraged horror to the skies, and generally violating the melancholy Dane's advice to the players. It should also be recorded that we heard Lottie Collins sing "Ta-ra-ra Boom-de-ay" and went home whistling the tune along the quiet streets.

The college haunt was the top gallery, standard charge per ticket twenty-five cents. The seats were long benches, no reservations, first come, first served. When a popular play was on we massed at the gallery door and when it was opened we stormed up the stairs like a herd of stampeding cattle. On one occasion I had the misfortune to be jammed against the door post by the mob and lost all the buttons off a new overcoat in the encounter. The boss of the gallery was a special officer, one Cowan. Armed with a long nightstick he sat in the back row and kept a watchful eye on his charges. Our signal that the curtain was about to go up was Cowan's shout: "Hats off! Gentlemen, please don't whistle." Sometimes we didn't.

In four years I saw a lot of plays, many of them bad, but our tastes were catholic and we liked them all. The college theater is now a part of the college and a useful part. The road company of the old days, playing the one-night stands and the tank towns, is a thing forgotten. While it lasted it was a good training school for actors and audiences alike.

Our growing sense of historical change had more foundation than the new things that we saw appearing on the campus. One impressive bit of evidence was the Free Silver campaign of 1896 that highlighted my junior year. That was also the year that I cast my first vote and in common with many others felt the stir of political awakening. By contrast, previous campaigns had been dull and spiritless, a threshing over of old straw, the Civil War, tariff, reform of the civil service, the iniquities of England.

The nomination of Bryan as the candidate of two parties, Democrat and Populist, was the culmination of a bitterness that had been growing through the farming West and South since the Civil War. Farmers had petitioned and complained, but to no purpose. Now they were acting. Their Peerless Leader was the man with whom they would march to the control of the White House and the Capitol, and his words were the embodiment of their own thoughts. To the East, Free Silver was financial heresy and Bryan the leader of a dangerous insurrection. All of us heard Bryan speak and marveled at the power of that magnificent voice. Only a man of iron could have followed the schedule that he set himself through the campaign, speaking ten to twenty times a day, carrying the burden of leadership alone, and traveling eighteen thousand miles to do it. Things are different now. Bryan belonged to the slow-motion era, local trains, cross-country jumps with horse and buggy, no jets, radio, TV. In 1960 one candidate covered seventeen thousand miles in a week.)

Our campus echoed the turmoil and the tension that gripped the whole country. We organized clubs to express our particular principles. We read "Coin's Financial School," the bible of silver advocates everywhere. If a greater campaign document than this has been produced I have not heard of it. We knew little of monetary theory, but we discussed it with the zeal and positiveness of the new convert. Here was a campaign that counted. In previous contests there had been rallies, torchlight processions, fife and drum corps "awfully arrayed," Roman candles, banners, and bands. In 1896 men were too grim, the issues too serious, for such circus performances. Men talked politics by the roadside, across farm fences, in street-corner groups. Preachers made stump speeches from their pulpits, and arguments sprang up in college class rooms. Country schoolhouses were forums for both parties, and families were split wide apart by bitter party differences. Whatever the verdict of history on William Jennings Bryan may be, he more than any other single man, made Americans politically conscious and articulate, and we saw it happening.

Some time in that year we staged a mock presidential contest on the campus, complete with parties, platforms, plots, deals, and stratagems. The liberals called themselves Federalists and nominated Theodore Roosevelt, newly risen to view as a fighting, reforming police commissioner in New York, as President, and Warden McLaughery, head of the Joliet penitentiary, for Vice-President. The opposition called itself Republican and nominated McKinley and some political unknown now completely forgotten. The choice of the Federalist candidates suggests that we planned a militant administration; at least it was a fighting campaign. The climax was the kidnapping of an important member of the opposition and locking him in a lightless, airless room in one of the buildings from which he was presently delivered in a state of near collapse.

A small group of us elected ourselves to the editorial staff of a campaign newspaper, which we dubbed *The Federalist*, published with the aid of a seedy old gelatine duplicating machine, with a crowing rooster at the masthead and a cartoon or two drawn by George Fitch. As journalism it was hardly a collector's item, but putting it together was a hilarious occasion. As was fitting we turned it out in the small hours, after the tumult and shouting of the day had died down, sustaining ourselves with milk and large slabs of raisin pie from a Main Street cafe. When the votes were counted the Federalists had a small majority, the losers shouted "Fraud!" and an uneasy peace settled over the campus.

Student imitations of a session of Congress in action were the vogue then, as student versions of the United Nations are today. One of these that was staged at Knox the year before I became a freshman impressed me mightily. The courtroom in the county courthouse across the street from the college was borrowed for the occasion as being mildly suggestive of the House of Representatives. The House routine of organization and procedure was followed as closely as possible. Officers were chosen, committees named, bills introduced, debated, and voted on. We might criticize congressional action, but we did not burlesque it.

At with our other activities, the members of the faculty took no part except as observers. We were educating ourselves and we required no help from professors in affairs of our own devising. Here lies the greatest difference between the college of that day and the present. Most of the other changes seem those of degree or of minor procedure, but with student activities the alterations are deep and important. Athletics, debates, plays, publications, all forms and phases of student life, so free and untrammeled in the nineties, have come under the overlordship of deans and committees, and student government is in constant danger of being only an extension of the machinery of administration. Doubtless there are fewer indiscretions and greater efficiency. "Activities Fees" paid into the college treasury finance these undertakings, and unpaid and overdue accounts are unknown. We followed the fumbling, experimental, democratic ways that had come down to us from pioneer times, making mistakes and sometimes learning from them. The change to organization and control—and careful bookkeeping—is part of the price we have paid for our growth in wealth and complexity. But it was the students who gave life and color to the older colleges, and few of us regret the parts we played. We entertained ourselves and not too badly.

The field of student activities was wide open. None of us knew of any faculty restriction on the number of "extra-curricular" jobs a student might choose to try. If we passed our courses we passed them and that was the end of it. What we did with the time we called our own was our own affair. In my senior year I edited the college paper, was president of my literary society, Gnothautii, managed the football team, took part in intercollegiate debating, then just coming into vogue, and was one of the senior speakers at Commencement. College work was easier then than it is now. I should add that I also managed the senior play, and the leading man and I found and hired the coach, a local printer who had been a trouper and knew more about staging eighteenth century comedies than the men who wrote them. If this sounds like boasting, it's because that's exactly what it is.

It was in our senior year that the sinking of the battleship *Maine* in Havana Harbor and the Spanish-American War that followed made the first break in American absorption in home concerns. None of us, of course, realized the importance of what was happening. All we saw was the drama of events, flags and uniforms and marching men. The great figures were Dewey at Manila, Teddy and his Roughriders. Captain Bob Evans of the *Iowa*, with his vivid phrase, "If I have my way Spanish will be the only language spoken in hell for the next hundred years!" All of a sudden, peace seemed a humdrum affair. The heroes of the Civil War were old men and their rambling stories of that remote past bored us. Now we had a war of our own at our front door, and we were prepared to enjoy it.

To be sure, we didn't exactly flock to the colors Some of the college men responded to the call and joined the local company of the national guard. Fighting Spaniards was more meritorious than standing guard against strikers, which was the only kind of military action we'd been hearing about. Most of us saw the war on the front pages of newspapers. Those who followed the flag spent dreary weeks in training camp, writing long letters home about the boredom, the rations, the heat, and the mosquitoes. Finally the local company sailed to the bloodless capture of Puerto Rico, to repeat there the boredom and the malaria that had already taken toll in the southern camps.

The rest of us turned out to celebrate when the news came of Deweys' destruction of the Spanish fleet at Manila, and speculated on the newly made admiral's chances for the Presidency. We read the vague rumors of the Spanish fleet that was about to bombard New York or Boston, or perhaps steam up the Potomac for the capture of Washington. That was a good war for newspaper correspondents. Banner headlines and long stories rested on nothing more substantial than the column of smoke that someone thought he saw somewhere in the direction of Cuba. Then we learned that there was a Spanish fleet and that Admiral Cervera had brought it boldly across the Atlantic only to hide it in Santiago Harbor. We thrilled when we heard of Lieutenant Hobson's exploit in sinking the old *Merrimac* at the harbor mouth to prevent the Spaniards from doing what our fleet outside devoutly hoped they would do, namely come out and be duly hammered to pieces. When Cervera and his fleet did just that in spite of the *Merrimac* and were promptly shot up by our guardians outside, we stayed up late again to shout our approval. Then the war was over and the class of '98 plodded through the Commencement festivities to the final day and the desired diplomas.

For me graduation was the sudden ending of the only life that I had known as a responsible individual engaged in definite tasks. For seven years I had worked toward that diploma and on the way I had tasted some of the sweets of campus fame. It was a small puddle, but I had been a considerable frog and I had enjoyed it hugely. Now that it was over my feeling was one of emptiness and lack of purpose Where did I go from here? What should I do? How could I bear the thought that this campus was my home no longer? I was only an alumnus henceforth, and that to me was less than nothing. The night after my graduation was dark and empty.

Six weeks later I left for New York and a magazine job that I hoped was waiting for me there. Henceforth I was to live in a different world and to travel new roads. When I next saw the college and the farm I had grown to maturity, I saw them with changed eyes and judged what I saw by different standards. The country I had known was changing, too, and was already strange to me as I was strange to it. The day I boarded a train for New York was for me the disappearance of the only America that I had known, an America that had been.